DATE DUE

JAN 21			

SPORTS
MEDICINE

GENERAL EDITORS

Dale C. Garell, M.D.

Medical Director, California Childrens Services, County of Los Angeles
Clinical Professor, Department of Pediatrics & Family Medicine,
    University of Southern California School of Medicine
Associate Clinical Professor, Maternal & Child Health, School of Public
    Health, University of Hawaii
Former president, Society for Adolescent Medicine

Solomon H. Snyder, M.D.

Distinguished Service Professor of Neuroscience, Pharmacology, and
    Psychiatry, Johns Hopkins University School of Medicine
Former president, Society of Neuroscience
Albert Lasker Award in Medical Research, 1978

CONSULTING EDITORS

Robert W. Blum, M.D.

Associate Professor, School of Public Health and Department of
    Pediatrics; Director, Adolescent Health Program;
    University of Minnesota

Charles E. Irwin, Jr., M.D.

Associate Professor of Pediatrics, Division of Adolescent Medicine,
    University of California, San Francisco

Lloyd J. Kolbe, Ph.D.

Chief, Office of School Health & Special Projects, Centers for
    Disease Control

Jordan J. Popkin

Director, Division of Federal Employee Occupational Health, U.S. Public
    Health Service

Joseph L. Rauh, M.D.

Professor of Pediatrics, Adolescent Clinic, Children's Hospital Medical
    Center, Cincinnati

THE ENCYCLOPEDIA OF HEALTH

THE HEALTHY BODY

DALE C. GARELL, M.D. · GENERAL EDITOR

SPORTS MEDICINE

Edward Edelson

Introduction by C. Everett Koop, M.D., Sc.D.
Surgeon General, U.S. Public Health Service

CHELSEA HOUSE PUBLISHERS
New York · Philadelphia

The goal of the ENCYCLOPEDIA OF HEALTH *is to provide general information in the ever-changing areas of physiology, psychology, and related medical issues. The titles in this series are not intended to take the place of the professional advice of a physician or other health-care professional.*

Chelsea House Publishers
EDITOR-IN-CHIEF: Nancy Toff
EXECUTIVE EDITOR: Remmel T. Nunn
MANAGING EDITOR: Karyn Gullen Browne
COPY CHIEF: Juliann Barbato
PICTURE EDITOR: Adrian G. Allen
ART DIRECTOR: Giannella Garrett
MANUFACTURING MANAGER: Gerald Levine

The Encyclopedia of Health
SENIOR EDITOR: Jane Larkin Crain

Staff for SPORTS MEDICINE
ASSISTANT EDITOR: James Cornelius
COPY EDITOR: Terrance Dolan
DEPUTY COPY CHIEF: Ellen Scordato
EDITORIAL ASSISTANTS: Nicole Bowen, Susan DeRosa
ASSOCIATE PICTURE EDITOR: Juliette Dickstein
PICTURE RESEARCHER: Debra P. Hershkowitz
DESIGN: Debby Jay, Jean Weiss
DESIGNER: Victoria Tomaselli
ASSISTANT DESIGNER: Donna Sinisgalli
PRODUCTION COORDINATOR: Joseph Romano

3 5 7 9 8 6 4 2

Library of Congress Cataloging in Publication Data
Edelson, Edward, 1932–
  Sports medicine.

  (The Encyclopedia of health)
  Bibliography: p.
  Includes index.
  1. Sports medicine. I. Title. II. Series.
RC1210.E33 1988   617'.1027   88-2568
ISBN 0-7910-0030-3
    0-7910-0470-8 (pbk.)

CONTENTS

THE ENCYCLOPEDIA OF
HEALTH

THE HEALTHY BODY

The Circulatory System
Dental Health
The Digestive System
The Endocrine System
Exercise
Genetics & Heredity
The Human Body: An Overview
Hygiene
The Immune System
Memory & Learning
The Musculoskeletal System
The Neurological System
Nutrition
The Reproductive System
The Respiratory System
The Senses
Speech & Hearing
Sports Medicine
Vision
Vitamins & Minerals

THE LIFE CYCLE

Adolescence
Adulthood
Aging
Childhood
Death & Dying
The Family
Friendship & Love
Pregnancy & Birth

MEDICAL ISSUES

Careers in Health Care
Environmental Health
Folk Medicine
Health Care Delivery
Holistic Medicine
Medical Ethics
Medical Fakes & Frauds
Medical Technology
Medicine & the Law
Occupational Health
Public Health

PSYCHOLOGICAL DISORDERS
AND THEIR TREATMENT

Anxiety & Phobias
Child Abuse
Compulsive Behavior
Delinquency & Criminal Behavior
Depression
Diagnosing & Treating Mental Illness
Eating Habits & Disorders
Learning Disabilities
Mental Retardation
Personality Disorders
Schizophrenia
Stress Management
Suicide

MEDICAL DISORDERS
AND THEIR TREATMENT

AIDS
Allergies
Alzheimer's Disease
Arthritis
Birth Defects
Cancer
The Common Cold
Diabetes
Drugs: Prescription & OTC
First Aid & Emergency Medicine
Gynecological Disorders
Headaches
The Hospital
Kidney Disorders
Medical Diagnosis
The Mind-Body Connection
Mononucleosis & Other Infectious Diseases
Nuclear Medicine
Organ Transplants
Pain
Physical Handicaps
Poisons & Toxins
Sexually Transmitted Diseases
Skin Diseases
Stroke & Heart Disease
Substance Abuse
Tropical Medicine

PREVENTION AND EDUCATION: THE KEYS TO GOOD HEALTH

C. Everett Koop, M.D., Sc.D.
Surgeon General,
U.S. Public Health Service

The issue of health education has received particular attention in recent years because of the presence of AIDS in the news. But our response to this particular tragedy points up a number of broader issues that doctors, public health officials, educators, and the public face. In particular, it points up the necessity for sound health education for citizens of all ages.

Over the past 25 years this country has been able to bring about dramatic declines in the death rates for heart disease, stroke, accidents, and, for people under the age of 45, cancer. Today, Americans generally eat better and take better care of themselves than ever before. Thus, with the help of modern science and technology, they have a better chance of surviving serious—even catastrophic—illnesses. That's the good news.

But, like every phonograph record, there's a flip side, and one with special significance for young adults. According to a report issued in 1979 by Dr. Julius Richmond, my predecessor as Surgeon General, Americans aged 15 to 24 had a higher death rate in 1979 than they did 20 years earlier. The causes: violent death and injury, alcohol and drug abuse, unwanted pregnancies, and sexually transmitted diseases. Adolescents are particularly vulnerable, because they are beginning to explore their own sexuality and perhaps to experiment with drugs. The need for educating young people is critical, and the price of neglect is high.

Yet even for the population as a whole, our health is still far from what it could be. Why? A 1974 Canadian government report attributed all death and disease to four broad elements: inadequacies in the health-care system, behavioral factors or unhealthy life-styles, environmental hazards, and human biological factors.

To be sure, there are diseases that are still beyond the control of even our advanced medical knowledge and techniques. And despite yearnings that are as old as the human race itself, there is no "fountain of youth" to ward off aging and death. Still, there is a solution to many of the problems that undermine sound health. In a word, that solution is prevention. Prevention, which includes health promotion and education, saves lives, improves the quality of life, and, in the long run, saves money.

In the United States, organized public health activities and preventive medicine have a long history. Important milestones include the improvement of sanitary procedures and the development of pasteurized milk in the late 19th century, and the introduction in the mid-20th century of effective vaccines against polio, measles, German measles, mumps, and other once-rampant diseases. Internationally, organized public health efforts began on a wide-scale basis with the International Sanitary Conference of 1851, to which 12 nations sent representatives. The World Health Organization, founded in 1948, continues these efforts under the aegis of the United Nations, with particular emphasis on combatting communicable diseases and the training of health-care workers.

But despite these accomplishments, much remains to be done in the field of prevention. For too long, we have had a medical care system that is science- and technology-based, focused, essentially, on illness and mortality. It is now patently obvious that both the social and the economic costs of such a system are becoming insupportable.

Implementing prevention—and its corollaries, health education and promotion—is the job of several groups of people:

First, the medical and scientific professions need to continue basic scientific research, and here we are making considerable progress. But increased concern with prevention will also have a decided impact on how primary-care doctors practice medicine. With a shift to health-based rather than morbidity-based medicine, the role of the "new physician" will include a healthy dose of patient education.

Second, practitioners of the social and behavioral sciences—psychologists, economists, city planners—along with lawyers, business leaders, and government officials—must solve the practical and ethical dilemmas confronting us: poverty, crime, civil rights, literacy, education, employment, housing, sanitation, environmental protection, health care delivery systems, and so forth. All of these issues affect public health.

Third is the public at large. We'll consider that very important group in a moment.

Fourth, and the linchpin in this effort, is the public health profession—doctors, epidemiologists, teachers—who must harness the professional expertise of the first two groups and the common sense and cooperation of the third, the public. They must define the problems statistically and qualitatively and then help us set priorities for finding the solutions.

To a very large extent, improving those statistics is the responsibility of every individual. So let's consider more specifically what the role of the individual should be and why health education is so important to that role. First, and most obviously, individuals can protect themselves from illness and injury and thus minimize their need for professional medical care. They can eat a nutritious diet, get adequate exercise, avoid tobacco, alcohol, and drugs, and take prudent steps to avoid accidents. The proverbial "apple a day keeps the doctor away" is not so far from the truth, after all.

Second, individuals should actively participate in their own medical care. They should schedule regular medical and dental checkups. Should they develop an illness or injury, they should know when to treat themselves and when to seek professional help. To gain the maximum benefit from any medical treatment that they do require, individuals must become partners in that treatment. For instance, they should understand the effects and side effects of medications. I counsel young physicians that there is no such thing as too much information when talking with patients. But the corollary is the patient must know enough about the nuts and bolts of the healing process to understand what the doctor is telling him. That is at least partially the patient's responsibility.

Education is equally necessary for us to understand the ethical and public policy issues in health care today. Sometimes individuals will encounter these issues in making decisions about their own treatment or that of family members. Other citizens may encounter them as jurors in medical malpractice cases. But we all become involved, indirectly, when we elect our public officials, from school board members to the president. Should surrogate parenting be legal? To what extent is drug testing desirable, legal, or necessary? Should there be public funding for family planning, hospitals, various types of medical research, and medical care for the indigent? How should we allocate scant technological resources, such as kidney dialysis and organ transplants? What is the proper role of government in protecting the rights of patients?

What are the broad goals of public health in the United States today? In 1980, the Public Health Service issued a report aptly entitled *Promoting Health-Preventing Disease: Objectives for the Nation.* This report expressed its goals in terms of mortality and in terms of intermediate goals in education and health improvement. It identified 15 major concerns: controlling high blood pressure; improving family planning; improving pregnancy care and infant health; increasing the rate of immunization; controlling sexually transmitted diseases; controlling the presence of toxic agents and radiation in the environment; improving occupational safety and health; preventing accidents; promoting water fluoridation and dental health; controlling infectious diseases; decreasing smoking; decreasing alcohol and drug abuse; improving nutrition; promoting physical fitness and exercise; and controlling stress and violent behavior.

For healthy adolescents and young adults (ages 15 to 24), the specific goal was a 20% reduction in deaths, with a special focus on motor vehicle injuries and alcohol and drug abuse. For adults (ages 25 to 64), the aim was 25% fewer deaths, with a concentration on heart attacks, strokes, and cancers.

Smoking is perhaps the best example of how individual behavior can have a direct impact on health. Today cigarette smoking is recognized as the most important single preventable cause of death in our society. It is responsible for more cancers and more cancer deaths than any other known agent; is a prime risk factor for heart and blood vessel disease, chronic bronchitis, and emphysema; and is a frequent cause of complications in pregnancies and of babies born prematurely, underweight, or with potentially fatal respiratory and cardiovascular problems.

Since the release of the Surgeon General's first report on smoking in 1964, the proportion of adult smokers has declined substantially, from 43% in 1965 to 30.5% in 1985. Since 1965, 37 million people have quit smoking. Although there is still much work to be done if we are to become a "smoke-free society," it is heartening to note that public health and public education efforts—such as warnings on cigarette packages and bans on broadcast advertising—have already had significant effects.

In 1835, Alexis de Tocqueville, a French visitor to America, wrote, "In America the passion for physical well-being is general." Today, as then, health and fitness are front-page items. But with the greater scientific and technological resources now available to us, we are in a far stronger position to make good health care available to everyone. And with the greater technological threats to us as we approach the 21st century, the need to do so is more urgent than ever before. Comprehensive information about basic biology, preventive medicine, medical and surgical treatments, and related ethical and public policy issues can help you arm yourself with the knowledge you need to be healthy throughout your life.

FOREWORD

Dale C. Garell, M.D.

Advances in our understanding of health and disease during the 20th century have been truly remarkable. Indeed, it could be argued that modern health care is one of the greatest accomplishments in all of human history. In the early 1900s, improvements in sanitation, water treatment, and sewage disposal reduced death rates and increased longevity. Previously untreatable illnesses can now be managed with antibiotics, immunizations, and modern surgical techniques. Discoveries in the fields of immunology, genetic diagnosis, and organ transplantation are revolutionizing the prevention and treatment of disease. Modern medicine is even making inroads against cancer and heart disease, two of the leading causes of death in the United States.

Although there is much to be proud of, medicine continues to face enormous challenges. Science has vanquished diseases such as smallpox and polio, but new killers, most notably AIDS, confront us. Moreover, we now victimize ourselves with what some have called "diseases of choice," or those brought on by drug and alcohol abuse, bad eating habits, and mismanagement of the stresses and strains of contemporary life. The very technology that is doing so much to prolong life has brought with it previously unimaginable ethical dilemmas related to issues of death and dying. The rising cost of health-care is a matter of central concern to us all. And violence in the form of automobile accidents, homicide, and suicide remain the major killers of young adults.

In the past, most people were content to leave health care and medical treatment in the hands of professionals. But since the 1960s, the consumer of medical care—that is, the patient—has assumed an increasingly central role in the management of his or her own health. There has also been a new emphasis placed on prevention: People are recognizing that their own actions can help prevent many of the conditions that have caused death and disease in the past. This accounts for the growing commitment to good nutrition and regular exercise, for the fact that more and more people are choosing not to smoke, and for a new moderation in people's drinking habits.

People want to know more about themselves and their own health. They are curious about their body: its anatomy, physiology, and biochemistry. They want to keep up with rapidly evolving medical technologies and procedures. They are willing to educate themselves about common disorders and diseases so that they can be full partners in their own health-care.

The ENCYCLOPEDIA OF HEALTH is designed to provide the basic knowledge that readers will need if they are to take significant responsibility for their own health. It is also meant to serve as a frame of reference for further study and exploration. The ENCYCLOPEDIA is divided into five subsections: The Healthy Body; The Life Cycle; Medical Disorders & Their Treatment; Psychological Disorders & Their Treatment; and Medical Issues. For each topic covered by the ENCYCLOPEDIA, we present the essential facts about the relevant biology; the symptoms, diagnosis, and treatment of common diseases and disorders; and ways in which you can prevent or reduce the severity of health problems when that is possible. The ENCYCLOPEDIA also projects what may lie ahead in the way of future treatment or prevention strategies.

The broad range of topics and issues covered in the ENCYCLOPEDIA reflects the fact that human health encompasses physical, psychological, social, environmental, and spiritual well-being. Just as the mind and the body are inextricably linked, so, too, is the individual an integral part of the wider world that comprises his or her family, society, and environment. To discuss health in its broadest aspect it is necessary to explore the many ways in which it is connected to such fields as law, social science, public policy, economics, and even religion. And so, the ENCYCLOPEDIA is meant to be a bridge between science, medical technology, the world at large, and you. I hope that it will inspire you to pursue in greater depth particular areas of interest, and that you will take advantage of the suggestions for further reading and the lists of resources and organizations that can provide additional information.

•   •   •   •

SPORTING TIMES

Sport of one kind or another goes back to the earliest days of civilization. What is remarkable about sports in our society today is not its vitality but the huge number of people engaged in it on so many different levels, in both team play and individual endeavor.

In the Olympic Games first held in Greece in 776 B.C., there was only one event, a foot race. When the modern Olympics were initiated in 1896, several more events were added, and still more continue to be added today, testing the human body further.

The body is not tested by sport alone. As people began to move from farms to the city during the Industrial Revolution of the late 19th century, their old ways of staying fit were left behind, too. Factory workers, including children, often worked 10 to 16 hours a day, returning at night to crowded slums in neighborhoods without parks. Over the course of a few decades, the evils of this arrangement gave way to the belief that physical fitness was vital to everyone's well-being. Robust good health, embodied at the turn of the century in the person of President Theodore Roosevelt (whose credo was "the strenuous life"), became the ethic of a whole generation, much as it is today.

Organized athletic events and contests, once the privilege of the upper classes, quickly spread to the middle and working classes—and the amateur athlete was born. He or she could be found competing in a grab bag of new activities such as basketball, baseball, and bicycling. By 1900, for example, the newly popular bicycle had become a prized possession of thousands of people in France, a sign of its owner's vigor as well as economic status. In the U.S. and Canada, immigrant groups organized softball leagues, church picnics at which games occupied the center of attention, and, perhaps most popular of all, gymnastic clubs based on European models. The emphasis in these clubs was on muscle strength and orderly activity such as marching, but by the turn of this century "physical educators" were emphasizing sports and games instead because they promoted team play and better motor skills (such as speed and coordination) and were more fun.

After World War I, a few highly paid professional athletes (most of them Americans) began to take the spotlight from other kinds of social leaders. With the advent of television after World War II, the salaries and the fame of hundreds of athletes grew exponentially. Sports, most of them still team oriented, flourished.

Was all the fun of sport and play in fact as healthful as regimented exercise? Apparently not. When America entered World War II, millions of draftees were rejected for being out of shape. After the war, a major survey of schoolchildren found that 58% could not pass tests of the basic movement of 6 muscle groups; in Europe, only 9% of the children failed the same test. Most team sports, so popular in America, were not as healthful as they were fun.

The new episode of fitness fever began in the 1960s. Jogging, marathon running, aerobics, the martial arts—all of these became part of the schedule of millions of people. But as more people took up exercise, more were injured, too. Injuries and their prevention became a growing area of study, and the modern era of sports medicine also began.

Sports and fitness have come to be regarded not only as a training ground for future accomplishments but also as an integral part of adult life. In high school and college, team sports build leadership qualities and foster a sense of cooperation that is essential for success in life. Many executives now make time for sports-based fitness programs, and there are people from all walks of life who do not feel up to par unless they break a sweat each day.

Whether fitness pursued on one's own or as part of a team is the better path to health is not the issue in this book. What is

Requiring strength, stamina, and quick reflexes, soccer is an excellent sport for overall fitness.

important is that physical activity of some sort be a part of every-body's daily or weekly routine. Injuries are a part of every athlete's life, so a better understanding of how the body functions when exercising, and how sports medicine can treat or prevent those injuries, will help even more athletes attain their fitness goals.

●　　　●　　　●　　　●

CHAPTER 1

· · · · · · · · · · · · · · ·

WHAT IS SPORTS MEDICINE?

S ports medicine encompasses a wide variety of specialties. It takes in simple first-aid and injury prevention, training, the right athletic equipment, adherence to a balanced diet, and a host of other commonsense applications. To be sure, on a more sophisticated level sports medicine also involves the use of revolutionary therapeutic drugs, surgical procedures, and machinery. But it is primarily an extension of many other, time-tested practices within the medical profession.

Almost every general practitioner is equipped to treat the minor sprains, bruises, and aches that plague the average athlete. For that matter, most parents can treat such ailments too, resorting to the family doctor only for their child's more serious injuries. Sports-medicine practitioners are called in when a more serious athlete needs professional care for the peculiar ailments asso-

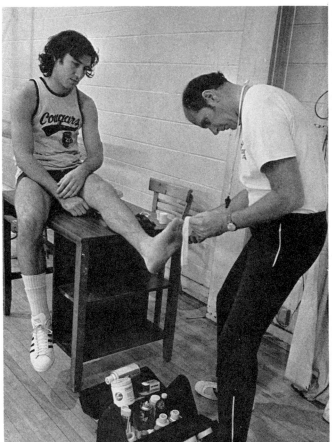

For many athletes, the team trainer is the first line of defense against injuries. He or she must have a sound general knowledge of conditioning and treatments.

ciated with long-term stress on certain muscles, joints, and bones. And such is the nature of sport today that the sports physician must treat injuries and recommend preventative measures never encountered by doctors in the past.

Filling a Need

In its purest form, sports medicine has long been available to the injured athlete. An Egyptian surgical manual written during the era of the Old Kingdom—more than 4,000 years ago—explained treatments for sprains and dislocations. Hippocrates, the ancient Greek honored as the father of medicine, described surgery to repair a dislocated shoulder, noting that "many persons owing to this accident have been obliged to abandon gymnastic exercises."

Not coincidentally, it was in 1898, around the time of resurgent interest in sports, particularly in the Olympics, that the first book in English on sports medicine was published. The International Congress of Sports Medicine was founded in 1928, and the American College of Sports Medicine followed, in 1954. These organizations portended the growth of a branch of medicine whose practicing professionals treat millions of patients yearly, in North America and abroad.

The reason for the astonishing expansion of sports medicine in the second half of the 20th century is twofold. First, people in the industrialized world, largely because of their relative wealth and greater amount of leisure time, have developed a passion for athletic achievement and competition, and with this passion have come injuries and strain.

Second, arising in part as a response to those injuries and in part under its own steam, the phenomenal advancement in medical technology has bolstered the development of the discipline. As the human body is better understood, everything from drugs to lasers to better shoes are put to work to heal it when it is in pain or to prevent injury from occurring in the first place. And this technology is available to more people than ever before, especially in the United States.

Sports medicine has filled a need: caring for today's more active person. The field came into its own in the 1980s. The American College of Sports Medicine now has more than 11,000 members here and abroad. Headquartered in Indianapolis, it has an active program of research, education, and certification of specialists. Sports medicine today is not only a respected medical specialty but also a billion-dollar-a-year industry. There are several hundred sports-medicine centers and clinics in operation and nearly 20,000 officially designated team doctors in high school, college, and professional sports.

Specialists The profession is composed of a multitude of specialists. In the more traditional line are those who practice arthrology (for joint injuries), orthopedics (for skeletal deformities, especially of the spine), and kinesiology (for muscles and movement), to name a few. Surgery is often a part of the rehabilitative process in these areas. Less specialized is the team trainer, who generally does more than train athletes to achieve their maximum potential—he or she also works with physicians and coaches to prevent injuries and treat them when they occur.

Sports medicine has its own basic research effort: exercise physiology. Exercise physiologists work to describe and explain the functional changes that occur during exercise. They examine the heart, the muscles, oxygen intake, body metabolism, and body composition. Their work has helped improve performance and curb injury by defining what the body is capable of doing.

Alternative Approaches Alternative medicine is a big part of the industry's boom. Just as sports medicine arose to offer what general medicine could not, such nontraditional and non-Western specialists as chiropractors and acupuncturists began to offer their services and now treat many champion athletes who swear by these optional methods.

The alternative-medicine group includes as wide a variety of specialties as the surgical field can claim. Some of them are as follows:

- Podiatry—the care of the foot.
- Physical therapy—the use of exercise to rehabilitate the athlete after injury.
- Osteopathy—the effort to restore structural integrity to a body somehow imbalanced by injury or neglect, which is accomplished by a combination of manipulation and regular medicine or surgery.
- Acupuncture—the use (based on ancient Chinese medical texts) of stainless steel needles inserted (without hurting the patient) into the body to relieve pain and disorder and to stimulate energy flow.
- Chiropractic—the manipulation and realignment of maladjustments in the body, such as in the spine, in order to restore normal nerve and body function.
- Nutrition—for an athlete's particular dietary needs.

The specialists in most of these fields primarily treat nonathletes, but all have come to the aid of athletes. Sports medicine has even incorporated some nonmedical therapies such as massage, psychology, and hypnotism.

There is a fair amount of resistance by old-line, traditionally trained doctors to the inroads made by the alternative practitioners, whose schooling is usually not as lengthy. As with any

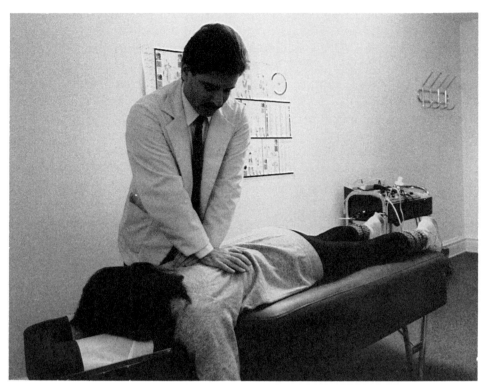

This chiropractor is one of the thousands of alternative-medicine practitioners whose contributions to sports medicine have helped many athletes perform.

growth industry, sports medicine has attracted some practitioners who are not completely qualified, and alternative practice is the easiest means of infiltration for them. A patient should always check the credentials of any doctor, traditional or alternative, before submitting to that doctor's care. On the whole, however, the increasing specialization of sports medicine is all for the good because some patients who could not be cured by traditional methods have been helped by alternative means.

In any case, the person who is just starting a training program should first get a regular checkup to learn if he or she has any medical condition that will preclude certain kinds of activity.

The Fit . . .

In the world of professional sports, the field of sports medicine has grown because world-class athletes today compete on a higher level than ever before. The demands of such intense training regimens on their bodies are incredibly punishing by past standards. Sports physicians, trainers, and members of many other disciplines are needed to help keep these athletes from exceeding their physical limits and to get them back into action soon after an injury.

A growing number of amateur athletes are also competing at higher levels. Just one example of the phenomenon is the tens of thousands of people who participate in the hundreds of marathon races run in the United States each year. At the 1987 New York City Marathon, for example, more than 22,000 runners joined in, more than 90% of them completed the 26.2-mile course. Just

The boom in athletic participation includes youngsters, too, who are also susceptible to Little-League or big-league injuries.

Being fat, or just out of shape, leaves the weekend athlete in greater danger of serious injury.

20 years ago, there were only a hundred or so participants. During the same period, the number of marathons run each year in the U.S. grew from 12 to more than 400.

It is little wonder that the public interest in preventing and treating sports injuries runs as high as it does. A recent poll found that 30 million Americans run or jog; 35 million play racquet sports; 14 million play football; 15 million play baseball; 15 million ski regularly; more than 6 million play soccer, and the list goes on and on. Young people are included of course: In addition to the 7 million American youngsters who take part in school sports programs, there are an estimated 20 million participants in out-of-school community athletics programs and another 20 million who play on their own—anything from sandlot baseball to weekend skiing.

Adding Inches, Shedding Time

The spotlight on injuries in professional and amateur athletics does little to discourage the participants from matching and exceeding the old records. These winning times and distances from the Olympics, and the percentage

Joan Benoit, gold medalist in the first women's Olympic marathon, at Los Angeles in 1984.

improvement over certain years, reveal the astounding achievements in a few fields.

The women's Olympic marathon was first held in 1984 and was won by the American Joan Benoit. Her time of 2:24.52 is approximately the time in which a man won the gold medal in 1956. At the rate at which women's times are improving, however, it looks as if women will take less than the 30 years men took to get from there down to the 2:09 mark.

And if these percentage improvements keep up at the pace they have in this century, we can surmise that in the year 2012 men will high jump more than 8 feet; women will swim 100 meters in 45 seconds; and marathons run in under 2 hours will be common.

To what limits will the human body be pushed in achieving these goals?

Women's 100-Meter Freestyle Swimming		
Year	Time/Height	% Improvement
1912	1:22.2	31.98
1984	:55.92	
Men's 100-Meter Dash		
1896	12.0 sec.	22.43
1984	9.99 sec.	
Men's High Jump		
1896	5'11¾"	16.75
1984	7'8½"	
Women's High Jump		
1928	5'3"	20.76
1984	6'7½"	
Men's 500-Meter Speed Skating		
1924	44 sec.	13.57
1980	38.03 sec.	
Men's Marathon		
1896	2:58.50	27.35
1984	2:09.55	

...and the Fat

The picture of seemingly relentless sports activity is deceiving. The truth is that a large percentage of Americans do not exercise regularly—and that includes young people. In a 1985 study, when children aged 6 to 12 were asked to do pull-ups, 40% of the boys and 70% of the girls could not do even one. When the U. S. Department of Health and Human Services compared body composition studies done on children in 1960 with those done in 1985, it concluded that the average American youngster was fatter and probably less fit than he or she was 25 years ago.

The lack of fitness creates a market for sports medicine, and it is the untrained athlete who is most likely to get hurt. At the other end of the spectrum, serious athletes who follow a rigorous schedule to prepare for top competition are also extremely vulnerable to injuries because their challenge is to get maximum performance from their bodies. In between are all those Americans who exercise regularly enough to suffer muscular aches and pains.

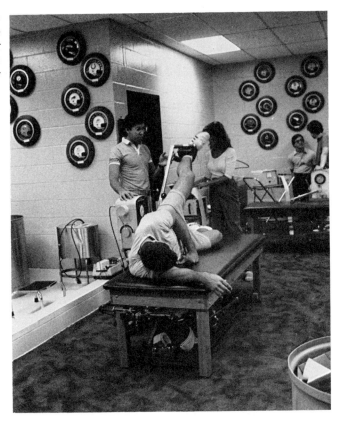

Staff members from a sports-medicine institute use high-tech equipment to measure the strength of a member of the New York Jets football team.

A Note About the Two-Class System

Of necessity, the care and treatment of professional athletes is on a different level from that required by spare-time athletes. Sports-medicine facilities for professionals are filled with hundreds of thousands of dollars worth of equipment—ranging from sophisticated exercise machines to whirlpool baths—that are not available to most amateurs. If a child who plays softball on summer weekends injures a knee, his or her treatment will likely be radically different from that given to a million-dollar quarterback who sustains the same injury. The underlying principles of treatment are the same, but the application of those principles is different when the athlete competes at the highest level.

Much the same two-class system exists within amateur or school sports. Athletics in this country's high schools and colleges are centered on a few team sports, primarily men's football and basketball. A player on one of those teams has a good chance of being looked after by a trainer who knows the basics about thorough preparation and injury-prevention principles. But not every school makes all of its training facilities and sports-medicine care available to women athletes or to the students who do not have the kind of ability or interest required for participation in organized sports. If you work out by yourself, injuries are always a possibility, and getting care when they occur becomes more of a problem. This situation is changing gradually as women's teams and the less-bruising athletic activities gain recognition. But disparities still exist. This book will try to offer information and advice for every kind of athlete or exerciser, though the reader is advised that some of the more complicated techniques of modern sports medicine are either not affordable or not feasible for every competitor.

The challenge for many people, young and old, is to get into shape without getting hurt. To do that, it is necessary first to know more about the human body and how it responds to different kinds of exercise.

•   •   •   •

CHAPTER 2

· · · · · · · · · · · · · ·

HOW THE BODY WORKS

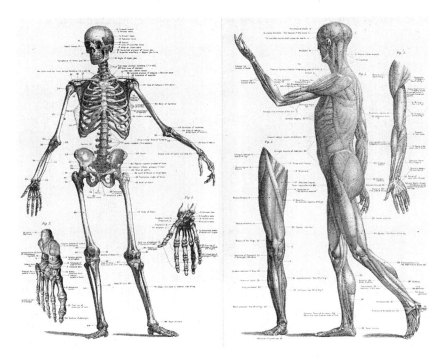

If you think of your body as a machine, you do it an injustice. The human body is far more complex than any machine. It has about 100 trillion components, or cells, each with its own library of genetic information that would fill hundreds of volumes if written out. Every cell has its specialized function, and cells are organized into larger components called tissues. Some cells last a lifetime; others have life spans measured in days. The body is constantly changing to adapt to its environment and the demands put on it.

Exercise is one of those demands, and the body responds to it in several ways. One way is to increase the supply of oxygen that goes to the muscles. During exercise, the muscles are put to work, and so they require more oxygen as fuel. They get their oxygen from red cells in the blood, which pick it up in the lungs and then carry it to the heart. The heart then pumps the oxygen-rich red blood cells to the rest of the body.

The Body in Exercise

One thing that happens during exercise is that the heart beats faster and pumps more oxygen-containing blood through the arteries, which are the blood vessels that carry oxygenated blood. Another thing that happens (in endurance exercise such as running) is that the body's control systems direct more blood to the tissues that need oxygen the most: the muscles and the heart, which is itself a muscle. If you exercise regularly for a prolonged period of time, the blood vessels feeding the muscles will adapt, growing larger in order to deliver more blood. The heart will enlarge also and will grow stronger, enabling it to pump more blood.

The muscles undergo the same kind of adaptation, but in a more complex way, depending on the kind of exercise that is

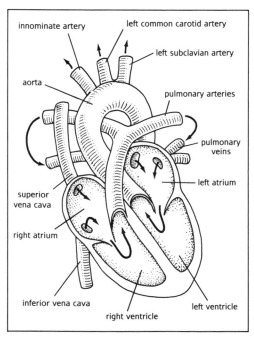

The heart, which pumps oxygen-rich blood throughout the body, is a muscle like any other that can be strengthened with exercise.

being done. To understand what happens to muscles during exercise, it is best to look at the entire musculoskeletal system—not only the muscles but also the bones to which they are connected and the tissues that connect the bones.

Bone Bone consists of a framework of a gristly protein called collagen and stiff clusters of minerals called bone salts, the principal one of which is calcium. Bone is usually thought of as something stiff and unyielding, but that is true only of dead-bone skeletons. Living bone is something else—it grows until adulthood.

Bone may change constantly if the body's needs and environment change. After a prolonged period in bed (or in the weightlessness of space) the bones begin to lose the calcium that gives them strength. During regular exercise the bones regain their strength and may also increase in strength and size in younger persons who eat and exercise properly. But bones do begin to grow weaker in persons of middle age. There is evidence that regular exercise can forestall this weakening and, with it, the fractures that are a leading cause of disability in older people.

Muscle Muscle is one of the body's many specialized tissues, accounting for about 40% of total body weight. Anatomists count more than 400 muscles in the human body. The function of these muscles is to contract and relax, pulling and pushing other tissues as needed.

There are three kinds of muscle: cardiac, smooth, and skeletal. The cardiac muscle, or heart, acts involuntarily in that it beats automatically while at rest; it is also classified as a voluntary muscle because it can be strengthened and enlarged through regular exercise.

Smooth muscle is mostly involved in such automatic body functions as digestion and is found in such places as the walls of the intestines and blood vessels. Smooth muscle is of little concern in sports medicine because, barring some unusual training, the average person cannot have much control over smooth-muscle functions.

The kind of muscle sports medicine is interested in is skeletal muscle, which makes up the muscular system attached to the bones of the skeleton. This type of muscle is also called striated muscle, so named for its striped appearance under the microscope. Skeletal, or striated, muscle is composed of highly organized arrangements of smaller fibers. This type of muscle is generally under voluntary control; it is stimulated by motor neu-

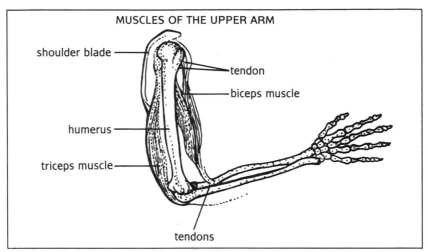

This illustration shows muscles paired in the upper arm: Depending on the motion signaled by the brain, either the biceps or the triceps contracts while the other relaxes.

rons, or nerve cells, whose cell bodies lie in the spinal cord or the brain.

Each skeletal muscle is enclosed in a sheath of connective tissue. Each end of a muscle is attached to a bone by a band of particularly strong connective tissue called a tendon. (We will discuss tendons in greater detail later in this chapter.) Most skeletal muscles are arranged in opposing pairs, meaning that when one muscle contracts, the opposing muscle relaxes. This pairing of actions is called prime movement and recovery. For example, consider the biceps and the triceps muscles, paired muscles located in the upper arm. If you want to bend your arm, motor neurons send a message to the biceps muscle to contract; as the biceps muscle contracts, the triceps relaxes, and the arm bends. If you want to straighten your arm, nerve messages cause the triceps to contract; as the triceps contracts, the biceps relaxes, and the arm is straightened.

There are two kinds of skeletal muscle fibers, descriptively called "fast-twitch" and "slow-twitch." Fast-twitch fibers contract rapidly and tire quickly. They are most important in such sports as sprinting, which requires quick, intense bursts of effort. Slow-twitch fibers contract more slowly but function for longer periods of time. They are important for such endurance sports as long-distance running. These runners may have a slightly higher percentage of slow-twitch muscles in their thighs, either inherited or as a result of training.

The difference between the two kinds of contractile fibers can actually be seen with a microscope. Slow-twitch muscles are fed oxygen by an ample network of blood vessels, so they are red. Fast-twitch muscles must work with only the oxygen they already contain for their brief periods of intense activity and so have no comparable blood supply; they are white. The body needs both kinds: fast-twitch muscles for speed and strength, slow-twitch muscles for endurance.

Cartilage One function of cartilage, another important component of the musculoskeletal system, is to act as a shock absorber between bones. Cartilage is essentially a pad composed of collagen, the same protein found in bone and also the chief protein in the skin and the body's other connective tissues. Cartilage is found at the ends of bones, particularly at the joints, where it serves as a cushion, allowing the bones to move against each other.

One key fact about cartilage is that it has no blood supply of its own, so it does not heal itself when injured. Though injury to cartilage occurs most frequently at the knee joint, cartilage can be damaged at any joint.

Tendons and Ligaments Muscles and bones are held together by several kinds of elastic tissues. For the purposes of

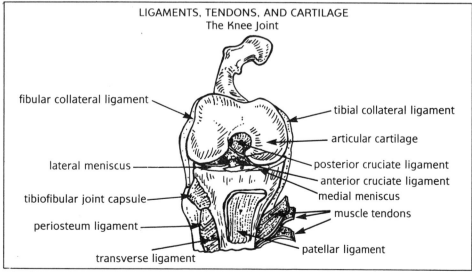

LIGAMENTS, TENDONS, AND CARTILAGE
The Knee Joint

fibular collateral ligament

tibial collateral ligament

articular cartilage

lateral meniscus

posterior cruciate ligament

anterior cruciate ligament

tibiofibular joint capsule

medial meniscus

muscle tendons

periosteum ligament

patellar ligament

transverse ligament

The knee is the body's most complex joint. Tendons, ligaments, and cartilage are the main components of joints, helping to connect bone to muscle and to cushion bones against one another.

sports medicine, tendons are the most important of these connective tissues. They are tough yet elastic bundles of fiber that anchor muscles to bones. They can be strengthened by exercise but are also subject to stress and inflammation and do not heal quickly.

The other kind of connective material forms ligaments, which are thinner bands of fibrous tissue that connect bones in joints. (They also serve to hold some internal organs in place, but this function does not usually concern the athlete.) Ligaments are pliant and flexible but do not withstand much extension and can therefore be torn when overstressed. Like tendons, the healing process for ligaments is slower than it is for a broken bone.

Joints Joints are complex structures made up of bones, cartilage, tendons, and ligaments, all contained in a package called the joint capsule. Nature works with two basic designs, the ball-and-socket joint and the hinge joint, but there are many variations on those themes, depending on the function of a joint. The hip is a rather simple ball-and-socket joint. The ankle is a rather simple hinge joint. The shoulder is a complex ball-and-socket joint, the knee a complex hinge joint.

Some of the most painful injuries, and those most difficult to heal, occur in the joints. They can become inflamed, extended, or can break down altogether if subjected to unusual strain over a long period. The knee is the largest joint, and as a result it is the one most commonly injured.

The Backbone Finally, there is that most important part of the musculoskeletal system—the backbone (also called the spinal or vertebral column). It consists in an adult of 26 bones, or vertebrae, that are stacked in the shape of a slight double curve. Viewed from the top, each vertebra looks vaguely like a fish with a hole in the middle. The holes of the vertebrae form the spinal canal, through which runs the vital tube of nerves called the spinal cord. A projection called the spinous process sticks out from the rear of each vertebra, and there are two other projections toward the side and rear called the facet joints.

The front portions of the vertebrae are attached to each other by intervertebral disks, which help give the spinal column flexibility and also act as shock absorbers. Each disk consists of an outer ring of tough cartilage and a jellylike core. The facet joints link the vertebrae, as do a set of strong ligaments. A powerful

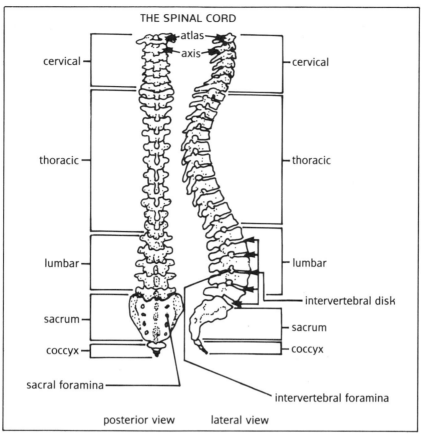

THE SPINAL CORD

cervical

atlas
axis

cervical

thoracic

thoracic

lumbar

lumbar

intervertebral disk

sacrum

sacrum

coccyx

coccyx

sacral foramina

intervertebral foramina

posterior view   lateral view

Composed of 26 vertebrae in an adult, the spinal column contains a tubular bundle of nerves called the spinal cord. Damage to any part of the column can be very painful and debilitating.

set of muscles running down both sides of the spinal cord help provide strength and stability.

Traditionally, the spinal column is divided into three parts. The top seven vertebrae make up what is called the cervical spine. This section of the spinal column has the maximum amount of flexibility. The next 12 vertebrae make up the thoracic spine. These are the vertebrae to which the ribs are attached. The thoracic spine is less flexible but stronger than the cervical spine. The bottom five vertebrae, the largest in size, make up the lumbar spine, the strongest and least flexible part of the spinal column. Its function is to support the entire structure. The adult spinal column also includes two single bones beneath the lumbar region: the sacrum and the coccyx.

In addition to its structural function, the spinal column also has a spinal cord, as mentioned, running through its center. At each vertebra, the spinal cord sends out branches of nerves that carry signals between the brain and the limbs and are affected if something goes wrong with the spinal column. They are susceptible to damage caused by slipped disks, arthritis, and other spinal-cord problems.

ENERGY FOR EXERCISE

Although muscles are made of protein, they burn either fat or carbohydrate when they need energy. Carbohydrate is the basic source of energy for exercise—specifically, it is the simple blood sugar called glucose. The body stores glucose in the muscles and the liver in the form of a molecule called glycogen. During exercise, a chemical change occurs in which glycogen is converted to glucose. The glucose is then metabolized, providing fuel for the muscles.

What happens when the muscles burn glucose is similar to what happens when an auto burns gasoline: Waste products come pouring out of the exhaust. The waste product of glycogen burn-

British distance runner Sebastian Coe. In long-distance races, many runners reach what is called the anaerobic threshold, which involves an oxygen shortage; some push even further and "hit the wall."

ing is a compound called pyruvate. During moderate exercise, pyruvate combines with oxygen to form carbon dioxide and water, which are disposed of by the lungs. But when exercise is too strenuous, there is not enough oxygen for that process to occur. Instead, the pyruvate is converted to lactic acid, which is not as easily disposed of. Because it interferes with muscle function and causes fatigue, lactic acid production is nature's way of telling the body to slow down. When too much lactic acid is present, the muscles will not contract. It is only when exercise stops that lactic acid converts to pyruvate.

The connection between pyruvate and lactic acid is responsible for some basic limits on athletic performance. When athletes gasp for breath, they are trying to take in more oxygen to burn up the pyruvate in their muscles. If athletes get enough oxygen to metabolize pyruvate, they are exercising *aerobically*. Trained athletes have worked up to a higher aerobic capacity than others. But when they exercise too strenuously, they reach the point wherein their body cannot supply enough oxygen to the muscles. At that point, they are exercising *anaerobically*, building up lactic acid in the muscles and reaching their limit of performance.

Athletes can tell when they hit what is called the anaerobic threshold. They feel breathless even though they are breathing harder. Good athletes in endurance events know when to cut back their level of activity to just below anaerobic intensity.

Hitting the anaerobic threshold is not the same as "hitting the wall," a phenomenon that is familiar to marathon runners. The anaerobic threshold is caused by a shortage of oxygen, which is relatively easy to replenish. "Hitting the wall," for a runner, on the other hand, means that the leg muscles have used up their stores of glycogen. The same phenomenon can happen to the arm-weary boxer: The glycogen in the arm muscles can be depleted. It can happen to the best-trained athlete. After his famous "Thrilla in Manila" fight against Joe Frazier in 1975, Muhammad Ali confessed that he could barely lift his arms when the last round started. That the arm muscles of the runner or the leg muscles of the boxer may have a goodly store of glycogen is to no avail because glycogen cannot be transferred from one muscle system to another.

Glycogen Storage Sports researchers can calculate when the muscles will exhaust their glycogen store. By those calculations, high-performing athletes routinely do the impossible. For example, leg muscles run out of glycogen after about 20 miles of steady running. Why is it that runners can complete the marathon distance of 26.2 miles even after they have hit the wall? There are several reasons.

One is that training can cause two changes in muscle performance. The first change is the increase of glycogen storage capacity. A world-class marathon runner might not hit the wall until 23 or 25 miles; a beginner may hit it many miles earlier. The second change is that exercise also conditions the body to burn more fat during periods of exertion, thus leaving more glycogen in the muscles for the final effort.

Another reason dedicated athletes can go beyond the limit is that even when glycogen is exhausted the body can keep going by using other energy sources, including protein. This reliance on other sources, though, can dangerously deplete the body's entire energy reserve.

Only the highly trained athlete should engage in this sort of exertion. The body builds up its capacity to run through the wall of glycogen depletion only when it is pushed frequently to the point of depletion. Depletion training obviously has its dangers and should be done only under proper supervision.

Glycogen creation and storage is just one part of the athlete's bodybuilding process. To stay in top shape, the body must get a wide range of nutrients to assist its physiological development. The right diet is the first step.

•   •   •   •

CHAPTER 3

· · · · · · · · · · ·

SPORTS NUTRITION

A premarathon pasta feast

The traditional picture of an athletic dining room is of a table lined with burly men who wolf down heaps of steaks, supplemented with vitamin pills and special pills that are needed to meet their unusual requirements. The emphasis is on protein to build up muscles—which seems logical because muscles are made of protein. And lurking nearby are self-appointed experts, ready to recommend esoteric kinds of diets and amazing supplements that will build athletic performance magically.

That picture of sports nutrition is one widely accepted myth. Another popular set of dietary myths connected with sports medicine concerns weight loss. Billions of dollars are spent every year in search of the one magic diet that will take weight off and keep it off. There are high-protein diets, high-carbohydrate diets, all-fruit diets—any conceivable kind of diet, sometimes (but not often) combined with a surefire exercise program that requires minimum effort. All these diets sell well for a time and then fade away, to be replaced by the next set.

Now for reality. There is an emerging consensus among nutrition experts about the kind of diet that Americans, including most athletes, should be eating. The "prudent diet" recommended by the American Heart Association to help prevent heart disease is remarkably similar to the diet recommended by the National Cancer Institute to help avoid some forms of cancer. This dietary consensus goes hand in hand with a consensus about the kinds of activities Americans should engage in to achieve physical fitness. There are provisos for special situations, such as athletes in intense training, but the exceptions are not that sweeping.

CALORIES

Calories measure the energy content of food. One dietary calorie is the amount of energy required to raise the temperature of a gram of water by one degree Celsius. The number of calories in a potato (about 90), for example, is a measure of the energy content it will provide. (The calorie is a very small unit, and frequently is replaced with the handier measure of one Calorie— capital C. A Calorie, or kilocalorie, is 1,000 calories, meaning that it can raise the temperature of one kilogram of water by one degree Celsius.)

Any person's calorie requirements depend on body weight and level of activity. A small person needs fewer calories than a large one. Someone who leads a sedentary life needs fewer calories than an active person. To a large degree, calorie-counting is straightforward arithmetic: If you put more calories into your body than you burn, you will gain weight, which the body stores in the form of fat. If you burn more calories than you consume, you will lose weight by metabolizing fat.

One problem with the way most Americans diet is that we focus on energy consumption and neglect energy expenditure.

Various diet books recommend a host of eating regimens for peak health. In fact, a prudent, well-balanced diet will provide all the necessary nutrients, without supplementary vitamin pills.

Common sense tells us that we can lose weight either by eating fewer calories or by burning more of them in physical activity. A combination of the two is healthiest and most effective. A 160-pound person who watches a lot of television will gain weight on a daily caloric intake of 2,500 calories, whereas a very active 160-pound runner can lose weight on 5,000 calories a day.

There are a couple of reasons why physical activity tends to be overlooked by weight-conscious dieters. One is that it takes a lot of activity to burn off calories. If you eat a candy bar and start jogging, it will take about half an hour to burn off the calories. And it takes 3,500 calories to burn off 1 pound of body fat—about 12 hours of swimming or 8 hours of tennis. In addition, there is some evidence that being overweight changes the body's metabolism, meaning that the heavier you are the more energy you have to expend to burn off weight.

Proteins, Fats, and Carbohydrates

The source of your calories also counts. The three basic sources of nutrients are proteins, fats, and carbohydrates. The calories provided by each of these groups are of greatly different value to the body-in-training.

Active people can take in more calories than sedentary people, who may gain weight no matter how little they eat.

Proteins are the structural units of the body; skin and muscle are made of protein. Proteins are long chains made up of units called amino acids. Our bodies can make some amino acids but must get others from food. Animal protein is the most balanced source, but it is possible to get the appropriate mix on a vegetarian diet.

Fats are an efficient source of energy because they contain a high number of calories per unit of weight, and they also carry some necessary vitamins with them. Hence, the body can call on its fat reserves for calories while it is exercising. The right kind of fat, however, makes a difference, for one broad distinction that heart experts make is between animal fat and plant fat, or high-density versus low-density fat. The difference can be explained biochemically, but it is visible to the naked eye. Animal fat is usually solid, whereas plant fat is usually liquid. It is plant fat (which is generally of low density) that is healthier to carry and hence useful to the body in exercise.

Carbohydrates are made up of sugars. There are simple carbohydrates, which are single molecules of sugar such as glucose, and complex carbohydrates, which are long chains of sugar molecules. A candy bar has simple sugars. Bread and potatoes have complex carbohydrates.

There are many misconceptions about proteins, fats, and carbohydrates. The image of the meat-eating athlete comes from an age-old bit of folklore: If you want to build muscle, eat muscle. In fact, a little bit of protein goes a long way. A typical American man needs only two or three ounces of protein daily to maintain good health. A nine-ounce serving of chicken or steak will provide that amount; so will three pints of milk. Several decades ago, the prevailing belief was that a lot of protein was better than a little. That belief has changed now, for science has shown that most Americans eat too much protein.

More important, it is believed that we also eat too much fat, and the wrong kinds of it, namely saturated fats (so-called because of their biochemistry) such as those found in red meat and dairy products. Though fat is an efficient source of energy, the saturated fats tend to get deposited in the blood vessels, where they can lead to heart disease. Most heart attacks are caused by the buildup of fatty deposits in the coronary arteries. The deposits eventually can close an artery completely, killing part of the heart muscle. Most foods that contain high levels of saturated fats also contain a lot of cholesterol, the intake of which has also been associated with heart disease; the less-saturated, lower-density fats from plants and white meats such as chicken and fish pose much less danger. New drugs can lower the level of cholesterol in the body, but it is still a good idea to avoid consuming too much of it.

The average American consumes about 40% of his or her calories in the form of fats, 40% in the form of carbohydrates, and 20% in the form of protein. Dietary experts would like to see us get not more than 35% of our calories from fat, 15% from protein, and 50% from carbohydrates, with an emphasis on complex carbohydrates. Though the recommendations are made with the prevention of heart disease in mind (heart disease is the leading cause of death in this country), they apply with equal validity to sports nutrition. (Surveys of the diets of top athletes, which reveal that many of them take in a wildly excessive and imbalanced mix of calories, indicate that these high-level performers have a great deal to learn about proper nutrition.) The mix of calories recommended for athletes, however, is designed to increase glycogen stores for energy over a longer period than that required by nonathletes.

Eating for Maximum Performance

The following important points for maximizing athletic performance and level of health are borne out by the large body of research that has been done on proper diet and good nutrition:

- Most athletes need a higher-than-average energy, or calorie, intake. The best sources for those calories are grains, dried fruits, breads, and pastas.

- Complex carbohydrates are vital because they contain minerals and vitamins, as well as the elements for the basic blood sugar, glucose. Simple carbohydrates, in the form of fruit, juices, and honey, are also valuable, although the simple ones in candy bars and other sweets are "empty calories," without other nutrients. Candy bars or other such stimulants actually deplete glycogen levels.

- A prudent diet requires neither protein supplements nor vitamin or mineral supplements. Women athletes do need to watch their iron levels, though, and vegetarians should consult a doctor about their special needs, such as taking B12 vitamins.

- Supplements such as salt tablets, bee pollen, wheat germ, amino acids, and other "magic-action" ingredients are generally considered unnecessary additions to a healthy diet.

- It is important to replace sweat and other fluids by drinking large amounts of water.

- Carbohydrate consumption and rest before an event will best replenish muscle glycogen.

Carbohydrate Loading Some athletes have adopted special practices to get an extra edge for intense competition. One such practice, popular with long-distance runners, is carbohydrate loading. The theory behind carbohydrate loading is that an ath-

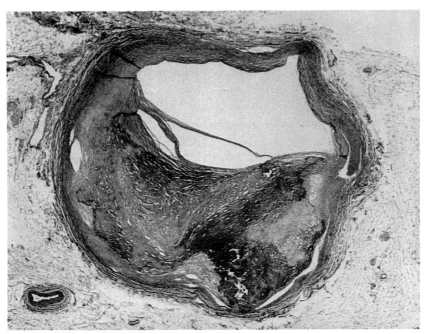

Excessive consumption of fatty foods can lead to clogged arteries such as this one, shown in cross section. Arteriosclerosis, the hardening of artery walls, is a leading cause of death among Americans.

lete can improve endurance by increasing the supply of muscle glycogen. The usual method of carbohydrate loading starts with an intensive workout designed to deplete muscle glycogen. That session is followed by three days of a low-carbohydrate, high-fat diet that maintains muscle glycogen at lower-than-normal levels. Three days before the competitive event, the athlete begins a high-carbohydrate diet and does only light exercise. That diet is maintained until the time of the event.

The practice can improve endurance in such demanding events as marathon races. The improvement comes at a price, however. The three days of the low-carbohydrate diet may be a time of irritability, fatigue, and body aches because the body's biochemistry is out of whack. And because carbohydrate loading causes the body to retain water, the athlete also experiences a temporary weight gain. Experts caution against the scheme. To start with, its practice should be limited to high-performance athletes who want to get the extra edge that could make the difference between winning and losing against top competition. Carbohydrate loading is thus not for the recreational runner. And it is definitely not recommended for anyone with a heart problem, because the high-fat diet may cause irregular heartbeat.

Whatever an athlete eats before an athletic effort, nutritionists warn that there should be a period of several hours between consumption of a substantial meal and strenuous exercise. The stomach needs an adequate blood supply to digest a heavy meal. To meet the needs of muscles, the body's internal control system reduces blood flow to the stomach during exercise. Lessened blood flow means that the food will be digested poorly, giving a lump-in-the-stomach feeling that does not improve performance.

Dehydration A measure that is much more questionable than carbohydrate loading is practiced by wrestlers, boxers, jockeys, and other athletes who must meet weight requirements for an event. They lose weight by a combination of starvation and dehydration, using saunas, hot boxes, and rubber suits. The American College of Sports Medicine warns that this practice has a number of adverse effects, notably reduced muscle strength, lower work performance, added stress on the heart, impaired body

Contrary to some advice, drinking water during and after exercise is vital for replenishing bodily fluids. Dehydration is a real danger for many athletes.

A Good Diet

Estimates of what constitutes a prudent diet vary somewhat, but most experts agree on the basics. The only difference between what an athlete and a nonathlete should eat is a slightly higher intake from the breads and cereals group for those who do a lot of endurance training, such as swimmers, soccer players, and especially long-distance runners.

The last category includes foods with more caloric than nutritional value; they are generally high in fats and sugars and should be consumed only in addition to the first four groups, never alone.

Food Group	*Servings	Principal Foods
Milk	3–4	Cheese Milk Yogurt Cottage cheese
Meat	2	Meat Poultry Fish Eggs (also beans and nuts)
Vegetables & Fruit	1	Vitamin C: citrus fruits and juices, melon, fresh berries, broccoli, tomatoes, etc.
	1	Vitamin A: carrots, broccoli, greens, sweet potatoes, apricots, squash, etc.
	2	White potatoes, other vegetables, and fruits
Breads & Cereals	4	Whole-grain and enriched breads and cereals; rice; various kinds of pasta; noodles
Extras	2–4	Butter, margarine, vegetable oils, syrups, honey, jams, other candies and sweets, desserts, carbonated beverages

*Minimum number of daily servings for young adults

temperature regulation, and depletion of the liver's glycogen stores. "It is possible for these changes to impede normal growth and development," the academy warns. (Contrary to athletic folklore, by the way, cold water is better than lukewarm water. The body absorbs cold water faster, which also helps keep body temperature down—a major consideration in helping prevent dehydration or exhaustion during workouts on hot days.)

For professional and amateur athletes alike, the American College of Sports Medicine recommends "a balanced diet . . . determined on the basis of age, body surface area, growth and physical activity needs." This levelheaded advice is endorsed by the mainstream of sports physicians. A sensible selection of items from the four food groups—fruits and vegetables, dairy products, meats (including poultry and fish), and grain products—will provide all the nutrients the body needs. For long-term good health, intake of saturated fats, cholesterol, and salt should be kept to a minimum. That is the common sense of nutrition for anyone.

Now that we have had a look at the physiology of the athlete's body, we will turn to a discussion of how sports injuries occur, what treatments they require, and how they can be prevented.

•   •   •   •

CHAPTER 4

SPORTS INJURIES

Sports injuries come in all varieties. Some are specific to a particular sport; others may plague anyone who exercises at all. The ladder of ailments extends from such minor maladies as blisters and sunburn to potentially disabling damage to bones and joints. In between are a few injuries that can seem insignif-icant at first but then develop into larger problems through im-proper treatment or lack of care.

Blisters Blisters form as a result of unaccustomed friction on a tender part of the body and are incurred by almost all athletes. They can be prevented either by toughening that part of the body by a gradual buildup of activity or by protecting it with gloves, extra socks, bandages, or another suitable covering. Most blisters should be left to heal by themselves.

Injuries from the Elements Summer heat and humidity are potentially dangerous because the body produces its own heat during exercise. In cooler weather, much of this heat is radiated from the body. In hot weather, the body relies on perspiration to cool itself, and the evaporation of sweat is diminished by high humidity. One piece of advice is to drink as much water as possible to replace the fluid lost in perspiration. Perhaps most important is to read the messages being sent by the body. Failure to heed those messages can lead to heat exhaustion or heatstroke, which at its worst can be fatal.

Heat exhaustion is caused by an excess loss of body fluid. Its warning signs are fatigue, weakness, and general malaise. These symptoms are a clear indication to stop exercising, get to a cool place, and drink a substantial amount of water or fruit juice. If such steps are not taken, heat exhaustion can lead to heatstroke.

Heatstroke means that the body has lost its ability to regulate temperature. Instead of sweating profusely, the person suffering heatstroke may stop perspiring, so that the skin feels dry and clammy even though body temperature shoots up to more than 100 degrees. Blurred vision, accompanied by dizziness, nausea, and sometimes irrational thinking, is followed by fainting if first aid is not given. The treatment for heatstroke is to get the victim out of the sun and lying down, with the head lower than the feet, and to pour water over the body or apply a damp cloth. The victim should drink water or, if unable, be given injections of salted water. Medical help is essential: Without proper care, heatstroke can kill.

Problems caused by the heat are more likely to occur in young children and older people because their temperature regulation mechanisms are not as good as those of young adults. Sudden heat waves increase the probability of problems because the body has not had a chance to acclimatize itself to the change in temperature.

Sunburn occurs when exposure to ultraviolet light is too great to allow the skin to build defenses by forming melanin, the pigment responsible for tanning. Dermatologists have become increasingly aware of the long-term dangers of sunburn. It not only causes the skin to age prematurely but also can lead to skin cancer, including the deadly kind called malignant melanoma. To doctors, a suntan is just a less severe, chronic kind of damage caused by exposure to the ultraviolet rays in sunlight, while a sunburn is an acute injury.

Despite the eloquent language used in advertising for sunscreen lotions, there is no magic to them. They prevent sunburn by absorbing ultraviolet radiation. The most effective absorbing chemical is para-aminobenzoic acid (PABA). Sunscreen packages now carry numbers describing their degree of protection. A sun protection factor (SPF) of 15 means that a sunscreen allows the same ultraviolet exposure in 15 hours that an unprotected person will get in 1 hour. Publicity about the hazards of sunburn has led to the marketing of sunscreens with SPF ratings of 30 or higher, but physicians say an SPF of 15 is enough for almost anyone.

The onset of frostbite is not always apparent to the person enjoying winter weather. Proper clothing can prevent it.

Cold weather also has its hazards, but it is possible to exercise during the winter by taking the proper precautions. Perhaps the most important safeguard is to dress properly, assuring adequate warmth without running the risk of becoming overheated. The best way to dress for winter sports is to wear several layers of light clothing rather than one or two heavy layers. This tends to prevent clothes from becoming wet with perspiration and, hence, losing their ability to insulate against the cold. Traditionally, winter athletes have worn cotton next to the skin to absorb perspiration and wool on the outside to give warmth and repel rain or snow, but a number of other materials, from down to synthetic fibers, have gained favor in recent years.

Frostbite can occur when an athlete neglects to protect vulnerable parts of the body—fingers, toes, and the head. When the body gets cold, blood flow to the skin is shut down in order to help keep the central core warm. If proper precautions are not taken, blood flow to an exposed part of the body is reduced to the point at which the flesh starts to freeze. The warning signs of frostbite are numbness and a paleness in the affected portion of the skin. Contrary to popular wisdom, the worst thing to do for frostbite is to rub the affected area with snow; that makes it colder and increases the risk of serious damage. Instead, the frostbitten area should be warmed gradually, preferably by immersing it in lukewarm (not hot) water. Reexposing a frostbitten area to cold air can cause added damage.

Hypothermia is a dangerous drop in body temperature caused by too much exposure to the cold. A major danger sign of hypothermia is confused behavior and slurred speech; the treatment is to warm the body rapidly, by immersion in a warm bath if possible. Properly dressed athletes are not in major danger of hypothermia, but the danger is real for those who exercise for prolonged periods in cold weather without being dressed for it, particularly for amateur mountain climbers and hikers but for skiers and skaters as well.

MINOR INJURIES

Moving up the ladder a rung to some more painful injuries, we find a group that any athlete can suffer. Inflammation, strictly speaking, is not an injury but the body's response to an injury, the first part of the healing process. Its symptoms are pain, reddening, swelling, and warmth. An injured part of the body becomes inflamed because more blood flows into it and body fluid leaks into the surrounding tissue. Inflammation can occur in many parts of the body. Perhaps the best-known kind of inflammation is tendonitis (-*itis* is the medical suffix for inflammation), which affects the tendons. But muscles and joints can also become inflamed. Bursitis, once called "housemaid's knee," is inflammation of any of the body's bursae, a bursa being a small fluid-filled sac located between a tendon and a bone. Bursitis usually flares up at the knee or shoulder. It was bursitis that ended the career of Red Rolfe, a star third baseman of the New York Yankees in the 1930s.

Arthritis is a general term for inflammation of the joints, which can be caused by nothing more than excess stress. Almost every person suffers from some degree of osteoarthritis, which is caused by the normal wear and tear that is part of aging; athletes are more vulnerable because they put greater stress on their joints. (Rheumatoid arthritis, usually a more painful, crippling disease, is caused by a still-unknown disorder of the body's immune system.)

Other minor injuries include sprains, strains, and bruises. A sprain is the result of a violently wrenched or twisted joint, resulting in torn ligaments and ruptured blood vessels and leading to internal hemorrhaging. Ankles and knees are the most common site of sprains, which can be caused by exercising without a proper warmup, overtraining a tired muscle, or by the unavoidable accident. Sprains can be minor enough to cause slight pain and swelling or severe enough to tear a muscle or tendon completely.

A strain, usually a less severe version of a sprain, results from undue stress or tension on one or more ligaments. Like a sprain, a strain can be minor or disabling. First baseman Jack Clark, then a St. Louis Cardinal, missed the 1987 playoffs and World Series after he severely strained an old leg injury during one wild swing of the bat.

A bruise, or hematoma, is bleeding caused by a blow to any part of the body; the discoloration seen in a bruise is the blood from ruptured vessels. Most bruises clear up by themselves, as the body absorbs the blood, but large, persistent bruises may need to be examined by a doctor.

Some back pains are a result of unbalanced use of muscles. Sit-ups or leg-lifts will strengthen the abdomen, taking some of the strain off the back.

Cartilage is also subject to injury caused by normal wear and tear. Injuries to cartilage can be troublesome because cartilage has no blood supply and so cannot repair itself. Cartilage damage is often associated with activity on hard or unyielding surfaces, which means that skateboarders, basketball players, urban runners, and many others can suffer from the pounding in their knees or hips. The prevalence of Astroturf, with its cement underlayer, accounts in part for the increase in joint damage suffered among pro and even college players in recent years, although it is difficult to quantify the contribution of Astroturf surfaces, as opposed to natural grass, to this problem.

Hard surfaces are not the only culprit. Even devotees of beach volleyball, who do squat jumps out of the soft sand, are known to have cartilage trouble in their knees and ankles. The joints in any hard-pressed body can give way, no matter the conditions. The back is also included in this list—the "slipped disk" that has caused so many people to suffer so much back pain is a form of cartilage damage.

Fasciitis is inflammation of the fascia, or the fibrous tissue that covers many muscles and tendons. It occurs most often in runners, who suffer inflammation of the plantar fascia, which covers the bottom of the foot, but it occurs in other sports as well. It can be caused by running shoes that do not provide good support, by overexercising, or by a sudden turn that overstresses the foot. Rest and anti-inflammatory drugs help the immediate problem; good running shoes, with inserts if necessary, can prevent a recurrence.

Unbalanced Use and Overuse

There are underlying physical factors to explain the occurrence of specific kinds of injuries in given kinds of exercise. If we look at the mechanics of the human body and the demands imposed on the body during athletics, we can see a clear pattern.

One common theme in athletic injuries is the unbalanced use of the muscles. As we saw in Chapter 2, the body's muscles always come in pairs, one muscle balanced against the other. Injuries can occur when an athlete overuses one of a pair of muscles while neglecting the other. The particular kind of injury depends on which pair of muscles is used in a sport.

Tennis Elbow Tennis elbow is a classic affliction of out-of-shape players that is due to improper use or overuse of muscles in the arm. There are two varieties, one caused by an improper forehand and the other, more common type, by a bad backhand.

The forehand kind of tennis elbow is seen more often in serious players, even professionals. It occurs when a player snaps the wrist forward too often and too vigorously, generally when serving. That motion strains the muscles that bend the wrist. They are attached to the inner side of the elbow, and that is where the pain is felt.

The backhand kind of tennis elbow is caused by excess strain on the muscles that straighten the wrist. It strikes players who do not use their entire arm when hitting a backhand but instead rely primarily on the wrist. The muscles that suffer stress because of this poor technique are attached to the outer side of the elbow, and that is where the pain is felt. It is estimated that 1 out of every 10 players will suffer from tennis elbow at one time or another.

The same kind of injury can be caused by throwing a baseball, a bowling ball, or anything else. The young person's injury called "Little League elbow" is one example. The attachment of the

Chris Evert-Lloyd uses a two-handed backhand to minimize her risk of tennis elbow, a muscle condition that may develop from overreliance on the wrist while stroking the ball.

inner-side muscle to the bone at the elbow is not as strong in growing children as in adults, so the muscle can be pulled away from the bone by hard throwing. When the injury happens in older baseball players, it is usually called "pitcher's elbow."

Hamstring Injuries The hamstring is a large muscle in the back of the thigh that lowers the knee. A pulled hamstring is another common injury and is caused by a muscle imbalance. In theory, a pulled hamstring can happen to any athlete. In practice, it occurs often in some sports, seldom in others, depending on the nature of the demands put on the body.

The hamstring is paired with the quad, a large muscle in the front of the upper leg that raises the knee. Hamstrings are pulled when the two muscles are not developed equally, meaning that the quad's force is too great compared to that of the hamstring. Sprinters and football players usually develop their quads more than their hamstrings and so are vulnerable to hamstring pulls. Bicyclists, especially those who use toe clips so that they are both pulling and pushing the pedals, develop both muscles equally, rarely pulling a hamstring.

Shin Splints One classic example of simple overuse of a part of the body is the set of lower-leg complaints that is lumped under the heading of shin splints, which fall into the class of ailments that start as minor but can become serious problems. They are caused most often by a combination of overuse and muscle imbalance. *Shin splint* refers to any severe pain in the lower leg, and it is the bane of athletes who run a lot, especially those who are just beginning a training program. Most shin splints occur when an athlete strains the muscle that pulls the forefoot up. This muscle, located in the back of the leg, can become inflamed. So can the membrane around the shinbone. And some shin splints are actually small stress fractures of the shinbone. The common element in all shin splints is pain that gets worse if the athlete keeps running. Wrapping the legs and resting them are the primary immediate treatments of a shin splint.

The pulled hamstring, bane of sprinters and many others, can come about from unequal development of the front (quad) and back (hamstring) muscles in the thigh. Carl Lewis missed several weeks of action after this pull.

Back-Muscle Injuries Though severe damage can be done to back muscles, most injuries there are minor, usually the result of imbalanced development. An athlete who does push-ups improperly, allowing the back to sag and not relying on a strong abdomen, may experience lower-back pain. The abdomen can be strengthened with sit-ups and other exercises, thereby eliminating some of the risk to the lower back.

SERIOUS INJURIES

Whereas injuries such as shin splints and tennis elbow occur because of muscle imbalance and overuse, many other injuries happen because the body is being asked to do something it was not designed to do. If unrealistic demands are kept up, injury of a more immediately serious nature may be done, including damage to the joints, bones, and musculoskeletal system.

Knee Injuries

Many knee injuries, although not all, are also a result of imbalanced use or overuse. The knee is built to combine flexibility with stability. Basically, it acts as a hinge, but a very complicated one. The knee is the meeting place of the femur, the main bone in the upper leg, and the tibia, the main bone in the lower leg. To provide protection, the kneecap is in front. A network of tendons connects the leg muscles to the bones of the knee. Five thick ligaments hold the bones of the knee together. Another two ligaments, called the cruciates because they cross each other, provide stability. The knee is lined with shock-absorbing cartilage, lubricating membranes, and sacs called bursae.

Football players suffer major knee injuries because the elements of the knee that give flexibility surrender some stability. Almost any component of the knee can be damaged if the leg is held still and the knee is hit hard. One or another of the ligaments can be sprained or torn completely. The kneecap can be dislocated. The cartilage can be crushed or torn. The bursae can be torn open. Bits and pieces of cartilage or bone can be ripped loose to float in the joint.

In addition to all this, the knee is subject to injury from overuse. The membrane lining the knee can become inflamed, producing excess amounts of fluid to cause "water on the knee." The

cartilage lining the kneecap can be inflamed, causing a painful condition called chondromalacia. Ankles, when similarly overused, can become partially or completely fused, requiring surgery to reinstate the right amount of space between the bones.

Shoulder Injuries

The shoulder separation is a hazard of all collision sports, especially football and hockey. The shoulder is a ball-and-socket joint. The upper end of the arm bone, the humerus, is the ball. It sits in the glenoid fossa, a socket-shaped part of the scapula, or shoulder blade, which is attached to the outer end of the collarbone.

The shoulder is built for mobility but has less stability than the knee. A shoulder separation occurs when the ligaments that connect the shoulder blade to the collarbone are stretched or torn. A minor shoulder separation is a partial tear that can heal itself in a few days if the arm is kept in a sling. A complete shoulder separation often has to be repaired by surgery, with the insertion of a pin to hold the separated parts together.

Anyone who follows baseball knows about the "sore shoulder" that pitchers so often suffer. It can often be traced to a set of three muscles collectively called the rotator cuff, whose function is to hold the humerus and scapula together. The physical activity needed to pitch a baseball can inflame or tear the rotator cuff. Inflammation can sideline a pitcher for a few days or weeks. A torn rotator cuff once meant an end to pitching careers, but sports physicians have now perfected surgical techniques that allow some pitchers to resume their careers.

Bone Injuries

The example of skiing can illustrate the agony of bone fractures because the sort of stresses put on the body by skiing make fractures common.

Three kinds of forces are responsible for most injuries in downhill skiing. The most common is external rotation, which occurs when one ski becomes fixed as the skier catches an inside edge. Momentum forces the skier forward and the leg is rotated because the other ski is fixed. If the binding that holds the ski to the foot does not release or the ski edge is not freed, the twisting force exerted on the leg causes a fracture of the leg or a sprain of the knee and ankle.

Cindy Nelson executes a sharp turn. Skiers suffer a whole range of injuries, from strains to fractures, in part because downward momentum can force unnatural rotation in their leg joints.

Gymnastics may demand the most flexibility of any sport, and most injuries in this field result from accidents rather than overuse or misuse of any part of the musculoskeletal system.

The second kind of force is the forward momentum that results when a skier decelerates suddenly or hits a large bump in the trail. The skier falls forward, bending the legs over the top of the boots. If the force is great enough, the Achilles tendon may be torn or the leg may be broken, in what is called a boot-top fracture.

The third force, internal rotation, is most common among beginners. It happens when the skier catches the outside edge of a ski or crosses the edge of the skis and falls forward. Sometimes the leg is fractured; more often the knee or ankle is sprained.

In skiing and other sports, there are two basic kinds of fractures: the stress fracture and the complete fracture. A stress fracture is a crack, but not a complete break, in a bone. These happen most often in the feet and legs and are an occupational hazard of runners. In a complete fracture, the bone breaks. In a simple fracture, the broken ends remain within the skin, and in a compound fracture, the skin is pierced. Obviously, compound fractures are the worst because they can lead to infection. But any fracture is one of the most painful injuries an athlete can suffer.

A compound fracture of the leg, occurring in a nationally televised football game in 1986 when Lawrence Taylor of the New York Giants fell on him, ended the career of Joe Theismann, the Washington Redskins quarterback.

Back Injuries

A major part of sports medicine is the study of how damage can occur to any part of the musculoskeletal system, of which the back is the most vulnerable component. One abnormality associated with back problems in athletes is a short leg. A common abnormality, short leg occurs because the body is usually not completely symmetrical. Problems can arise when one leg is more than a half-inch shorter than the other. When someone with a short leg does a lot of running, more stress is put on one side of the body. The spine curves to compensate for the stress, putting unequal pressure on the disks, muscles, and ligaments of the spinal column. The eventual result can be disabling pain. The remedy is a shoe insert that equalizes leg lengths.

Back problems in athletes are just variations on the kind of back trouble suffered by many nonathletes. For example, a football player may suffer a strain of the cervical spine (the uppermost part of the spinal column) after a powerful hit on the shoulders. That injury is the same as the whiplash suffered in an auto accident, when the spinal column is whipped backward suddenly. A slipped disk—actually the protrusion of part of a disk from the spinal column—can happen to a weight lifter or a football player, but it also strikes those doing housework or yardwork.

Slipped vertebrae in the lumbar spine (the lower back) do appear to be more common in several sports, including football and gymnastics. A weekend tennis player can suffer back spasms as muscles tighten when the body is twisted. Anyone who rides a racing bicycle can suffer back pain when bending over the handlebars.

Great strides in the treatment of sports injuries have been made in recent years. As it has developed training techniques to extend the frontiers of human achievement and warmup regimens to minimize the risk of injuries, sports medicine has also initiated better treatment methods for professionals and amateurs alike.

CHAPTER 5

TREATING SPORTS INJURIES

Just as sports injuries can range from the minor to the major, the treatment of them can run from the commonsensical to the futuristic. Most can be managed on the spot by the athlete, but care must be taken to avoid aggravating the problem. This chapter will examine how sports medicine today has come to include some very technologically sophisticated procedures. It will also show how and to what degree most amateur athletes can rely on self-care and care by nonspecialists.

Injuries and Warning Signs

Self-treatment of minor injuries has its limits. There are warning signs of serious injury that should not be ignored and that call for a visit to a physician.

The most obvious one is persistent pain, which is nature's way of saying that something has gone wrong. Persistent pain, especially pain that gets worse during exercise, calls for medical attention. In particular, pain in a bone or joint for more than two weeks often indicates a serious injury. An injured joint should be kept immobilized until it is examined. Left untreated, joint injuries can cause permanent disability.

Another warning sign is loss of function, or an inability to use part of the body. The duration of a minor injury is also important: If it persists, the injury may not be minor at all. For example, a sprained finger should start getting better in two or three days. If it remains discolored, immobile, and painful, the cause could be a broken bone, not a sprain. Anyone suffering what appears to be a broken bone should keep that part of the body immobile until medical help arrives. Well-meaning people who try to rush a patient to the hospital can make a fracture much worse than if they waited for professional aid. The patient should be moved with care, preferably by trained people. When they are properly set, bone breaks almost always heal themselves adequately.

If someone who has been hit in the head appears confused or dazed, a concussion should be suspected. A concussion results from a jarring blow to the head and can mean temporary or even permanent disturbance in cerebral function; it can be thought of metaphorically as a severe bruising of the brain. Immediate evaluation by a doctor is required, and if the athlete has been knocked unconscious, he or she should not be moved, unless breathing is impaired and resuscitation is necessary.

The same advice applies to major neck injuries because of the risk of injury to the spinal cord. Most neck injuries carry no such risk, but they can be extremely painful. Muscle spasms are common in the neck. They can be severe enough to set the head off at an angle. In an effort to prevent this condition, called spastic torticollis, people wear cervical collars to keep the injured area immobilized. Heat, anti-inflammatory drugs, muscle relaxants, and a gentle program of muscle-stretching exercises can overcome the problem.

The big problem with the abdomen in sports is a pulled abdominal muscle, or strain. It gets the standard treatment, with ice and rest at first, heat later. Abdominal pulls are indications that the muscles are not in shape, so an exercise program to strengthen them usually is in order.

The RICE System

Immediate treatment of minor sports injuries is called RICE, after its four components: rest, ice, compression, and elevation. It is recommended for any injury serious enough to call attention to itself.

Rest means simply stopping exercise. Playing with a small injury can make it a big one. Rest does not have to mean total immobilization for an athlete, however. Usually, it is only the injured part that has to be rested. If the elbow is injured, running is still possible. If a foot is injured, swimming may be possible. The amount of rest depends on the extent of the injury; it can range from a few minutes to a few days.

Ice is applied to the injured area for several reasons. It gives some immediate relief because it deadens pain. It also reduces bleeding by causing blood vessels to contract and lessens swelling and inflammation by reducing the amount of fluid released from injured tissue as part of the body's response to trauma. Ethylene

Ice deadens pain; it lessens swelling by reducing the fluid in the traumatized area; and it reduces bleeding by causing blood vessels to contract.

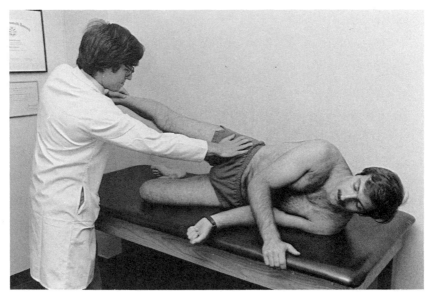

An orthopedic surgeon may recommend a range of treatments to the patient, including ultrasound or diathermy, exercises, and surgery.

glycol, which reduces pain by freezing the spot, is the active ingredient in sprays applied to a bruise from a fall or from being hit with a baseball, racquetball, or the like.

Ice should not be applied directly to the skin. It should be wrapped in a towel or cloth and then applied for 15 to 20 minutes at a time.

Compression also helps reduce swelling and inflammation. For most minor injuries, it is enough to wrap an elastic bandage around the injured area. The bandage can be wrapped over the ice. If there is numbness and pain when the bandage is applied, it should be loosened a bit. Because almost all injured areas swell somewhat, the fit of the bandage should be checked regularly.

Elevation is another strategy for minimizing inflammation and swelling. If the injured part is elevated, gravity will drain fluid away from it. The elevation does not have to be extreme. Keeping an injured foot on a pillow or two can be enough.

Heat Treatments Whereas cold is good for immediate treatment of an injury, heat is good later on, during the period of repair and rehabilitation. Bruises are treated immediately with ice to limit the bleeding and later with heat to promote blood absorption. Heat helps in the rehabilitation process in several ways, notably by increasing blood flow and relaxing muscles.

Liniments (medicinal preparations that are rubbed on the skin) can provide heat, but their effect is literally superficial because they do not penetrate deeply into the body.

Another way to apply heat is to use a hydrocollator, a pack containing a silicon-and-sand gel that absorbs water. The hydrocollator is immersed in hot water, wrapped in one or more towels, and applied to the injured area for about 20 minutes.

Professional therapists use diathermy machines for heat treatments. There are several varieties of diathermy, including ultrasound, which we will discuss in greater detail later in this chapter, and microwave devices. All work on the same principle: beaming energy deep into the body.

The RICE system can cover a lot of ground if used correctly. A muscle pull in a younger person, depending on its severity, will heal in a few days to a few weeks if ministered to quickly upon injury. The healing time gets longer with age. When lessened pain indicates that the healing process has begun, stretching exercises should be started to slowly strengthen the muscle. And the treatment for most cases of tennis elbow is mainly rest, sometimes including a sling if the pain is bad enough.

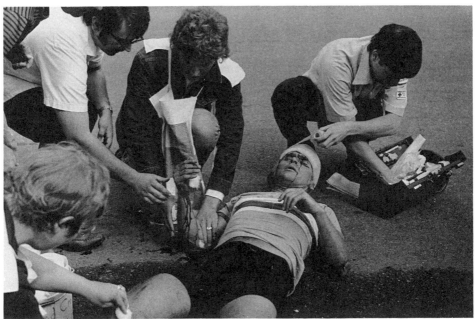

Victims of serious injury, especially to the head, neck, or back, should not be moved until professional help arrives, unless resuscitation is necessary.

New Directions in Treatment

Advances in medical technology in the last two decades have provided sports physicians with an array of techniques for healing the fallen athlete. One technique is ultrasound, the directed use of high-frequency sound waves on an injured interior tissue, such as for Achilles tendonitis. In an ultrasound treatment, plates attached to wires are wrapped around the affected area, and the sound waves are beamed directly at the wound. The waves heat and stimulate the tissue of the surrounding area and break up internal scar tissue. The treatment has the effect of a deep massage, increasing blood flow and relaxing the strained joint.

Arthroscopy Methods once reserved for professionals are now being used to help weekend athletes as well. One of the most impressive is arthroscopic surgery. Arthroscopy is a technique that enables doctors to repair many joint injuries, especially to the knee, without major surgery. In arthroscopy, a hollow tube containing a miniature television camera is inserted in the joint through an incision less than an inch long. An image of the joint's interior is projected on a television screen. The physician uses a specially designed set of instruments to operate on the injured part—repairing or cutting away damaged cartilage, for example, or stitching in new tendon fibers. Recovery time is measured in days rather than in the weeks needed after conventional surgery, in which more disruption is caused to the injured area.

In 1976, Tommy John was told that his career as a major league pitcher was over because of a torn rotator cuff in his shoulder, an injury from which no pitcher had ever come back. John underwent arthroscopic surgery performed by one of the most renowned sports physicians, Dr. Frank Jobe of Los Angeles. In what at the time was described as nearly a miracle, John's shoulder was rebuilt. He was still pitching for the New York Yankees in 1987.

Transplants In an even more astounding development, it is now possible to transplant the entire donated knee joint of one person into another person. The first operation of this kind was performed in 1987 on a woman with a malignant tumor in her knee. After doctors removed the tumor and 16 inches of adjoining bone, the new joint was attached with the aid of metal rods and screws to fix it to the patient's femur, fibula, and tibia. In an operation that took about seven hours, a new kneecap and a

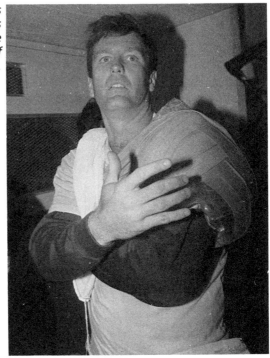

Pitcher Tommy John's torn rotator cuff was repaired through the modern technique of arthroscopic surgery.

dozen ligaments and tendons were also implanted. The surgery was all the more miraculous because, though it was the first joint transplant ever done, it involved the body's largest and most complicated joint.

This kind of operation cannot yet be expected to restore perfect coordination and mobility to the injured person. But it does hold out hope for the rare athlete with a joint so completely and irreparably damaged that a new one is the only solution. It is doubtful whether a transplanted joint would ever restore a triathlete to the field of competition, but it would allow him or her to lead a normal life without intensive exercise. Because of the expense of the procedure, it is also likely that it will be performed only in emergency situations or on the most highly paid professional athletes.

Other New Developments As advances are made in science and technology, many of them are being applied to sports medicine. Because the unbalanced use of muscles is a major source of injury, techniques for observing the athlete in motion are a key to devising new methods of prevention and treatment.

One recent development is high-speed cinematography, which allows, for example, the sprint and takeoff of a pole-vaulter to be filmed for slow-motion viewing. By capturing every step of the athlete's vital movements, the film isolates flaws leading to poor performance or to strain on certain muscles or joints. Other gear used for similar purposes includes cable tensiometers, to measure whether muscles are being used complementarily, and force plates, to quantify the exertion of each muscle group.

The Surgery Option

Although certain surgical procedures are quite valuable, the publicity given to them can nevertheless obscure the less dramatic but equally important progress made in the treatment of the majority of ordinary sports injuries. This progress is being made not so much by the development of drastically new technology but through everyday application of the facts that sports physicians have learned about the capabilities of the human body and the factors that lead to injuries. Today's treatments by kinesiologists, physical therapists, chiropractors, and a host of others is more straightforward, usually including a prescription of exercise and advice on how to prevent recurrences.

These humbler approaches are in fact the choice of some of the world's top athletes, who cannot or will not be laid up after surgery for fear of losing their peak condition. John Howard, who holds the world speed record for paced cycling—152.84 miles per hour—is one who balked at the idea of surgery. He suffered a painful debility, familiar to many bikers, called carpal-tunnel syndrome, in which nerves in the wrists are pinched and the hands consequently become dysfunctional from the pounding they take on the handlebars. "I used heat and ice at the beginning," he said, "then squeezed rubber balls constantly for about a year." He gradually regained use of his hands, but at a price to his cycling supremacy: He has had to decrease his daily mileage, wear padded gloves, and use handlebar grips.

Physical manipulation has also helped thousands of athletes, professional and amateur, overcome an injury without resorting to surgery. Manipulation can take many forms: massage from the team trainer; deep-friction massage, which is also known as acupressure in the Western world and shiatsu in the Orient; or chiropractic, to name a few. The purpose is to strengthen and rehabilitate the body as the injury itself heals. Leg weights are a common means of strengthening the quad muscles in the upper leg after a knee injury, to insure that no undue strain is put upon the knee when the athlete returns to action.

There are times when surgery is necessary. Joanne Ernst, a top triathlete, had torn tendons in her right hamstring, making running very difficult and cycling extremely painful. She underwent an operation in which the sheaths around the affected tendons were removed, and she hopes to compete in the 1988 Olympics after a rehabilitation program that will strengthen the adjacent and complementary tendons and ligaments.

Marathon runner Alberto Salazar is another who resisted surgery but had to give in. He was the best marathoner in the world in 1981–83 (winning the 1981 New York City Marathon in 2:08:13), but had to have repeated surgery on his legs because of a host of knee and tendon problems that failed to respond to nonsurgical treatment. He eventually discovered that he had an iron deficiency as well. Asked to explain his many ailments, he said, "[My podiatrist, chiropractor, and I] think the problem is biomechanical. After all my leg injuries, the resulting compensations, the surgeries, I'm just not running with my old form. A couple of months ago we found a quarter-inch leg length discrepancy. I tried an orthotic (an insert in the shoe that supports the arch) in my left shoe, and we just doubled its height. I'm hoping that does it."

To be sure, surgery is a more radical treatment than manipulation, but manipulation itself is far from painless. In cases that seem to require one or the other form of intervention, the athlete can consult at least one appropriate sports physician and together they can arrive at a suitable short- or long-term treatment and recovery schedule.

The Right Equipment

In the aftermath of treatment for a sports injury, many athletes rethink their immortality and give in to the idea that certain precautions can become a permanent and painless part of recovery. Along with sensible training, the right equipment can help. Starting at the top, the eyes deserve special attention but often do not get it, perhaps because many athletes think protective gear interferes with their sight. Kareem Abdul-Jabbar does

Basketball great Kareem Abdul-Jabbar has worn protective eye goggles for many years.

not think so; he started wearing goggles after a finger was poked in his eye.

The eyes should be protected when playing any racquet sport. Ordinary eyeglasses or sunglasses with safety lenses and impact-resistant frames are generally good enough for tennis, where the ball is relatively soft and large. For racquetball, where the ball is hard and moves more rapidly, goggles or the equivalent are needed; for hockey, a visor is recommended.

At the other end, good athletic shoes are a must for any sport that requires a lot of running. When a runner is in full stride, each foot absorbs more than seven times the body weight with each stride. Good shoes help cushion the impact. A good athletic shoe should have a well-padded tongue and Achilles pad (the cushion at the top of the heel), a raised heel wedge, and good arch support. The midsole should be flexible, and the end should allow room to wiggle the toes.

One problem that affects many athletes is excessive pronation, inward turning of the feet. The feet normally turn in slightly during running, as weight is transferred from the heel to the toes during each stride. An excessive inward turn can lead to pain and inflammation in the toe or heel and eventually cause trouble with the ankles, knees, and hips. One way to detect excessive pronation is to look at the soles of the running shoes; abnormal wear on the inner side of the sole is a sign of trouble. Corrective surgery is a solution to this maladjustment in rare cases, but an easier way is to wear special shoes or orthotics, the inserts that Alberto Salazar is using to correct his short-leg problem.

Knee braces can help impede further injury to damaged knees, although their value in preventing knee injuries altogether has not been proven. A 1987 study of high school football players found no reduction in knee injuries in those who wore braces. A good brace does, however, provide extra support for a knee made unstable by injury. A good brace is not cheap. The most popular brace used by professional athletes, developed at Lenox Hill Hospital in New York, is custom-made and costs at least

Knee braces are worn by many of today's athletes, amateur and professional, either after surgery or as insurance against injury while they play. The principle is to provide mobility as well as stability.

$400. It has been worn by pro quarterbacks Joe Namath, Dan Marino, and Dan Fouts, among others.

In general, many sports injuries are minor enough to be handled by rest or by cutting back a bit on training. Some athletes take what they think is a quick way around lengthy recuperation by taking drugs. The many new drugs on the market are surely a boon to sports medicine and a great help to doctors as well, who in some cases may be as reluctant as the athlete is to turn to surgery or other delicate procedures on the injured body. Drugs can also be abused, however, both recreationally and medically. Their role in treating sports injuries and enhancing athletic performance is a subject every modern athlete must understand.

•   •   •   •

CHAPTER 6

• • • • • • • • • • • • •

DRUG THERAPY AND ABUSE

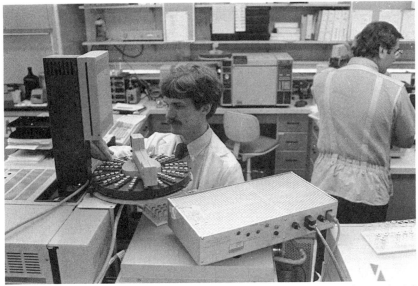

A drug-testing lab

Perhaps the most disturbing recent development in sports medicine is the use and abuse of drugs by athletes. The drug problem in sports falls into three categories. One is the illegal, recreational use of such street drugs as cocaine by athletes off the field. The second is the use of a variety of drugs, most of them available legally, to enhance performance. The third is inappropriate drug use for pain relief. All three practices seem to have become increasingly common. Many sports physicians are poorly equipped to handle the drug problem. Indeed, there have been frequent charges that some physicians are part of the problem because they themselves provide athletes with prescription drugs such as amphetamines and steroids.

Testing for performance-enhancing drugs has become an unhappily routine part of major athletic competitions, up to and including the Olympics, and a number of athletes have been disqualified when they tested positive. Use of performance-enhancing drugs has been reported in all areas of organized sports, in some cases down to the high school level.

The same is true of such so-called recreational drugs as cocaine. The prominent athletes whose careers have been disrupted by cocaine include Keith Hernandez, Dwight Gooden, Dave Parker, and Steve Howe in baseball alone; in basketball, cocaine was responsible for the death of Len Bias, the first-round draft choice of the Boston Celtics in 1986. In football, Mercury Morris of the Miami Dolphins and Thomas "Hollywood" Henderson of the Dallas Cowboys are among those whose careers were shortened by cocaine use. Street-drug abuse in sports, in both the professional and the amateur arena, is only part of a larger problem in our society.

New York Mets pitcher Dwight Gooden went briefly to the minor leagues to regain his form after a 6-week drug rehabilitation program. Cocaine use is a major problem in professional athletics as well as in society at large.

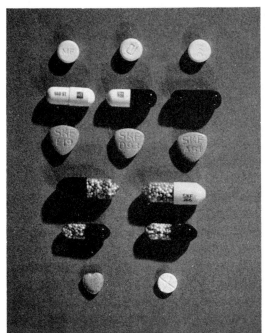

A wide variety of amphetamines have been used by athletes wishing to artificially enhance their performance. But "uppers" have various harmful side effects and can be addictive.

PERFORMANCE-ENHANCING DRUGS

Although drug abuse among athletes is not new, the problem is more severe now than it was even 30 years ago. The extent of the problem is indicated by the list of drugs banned for Olympic athletes. It includes psychomotor-stimulating drugs such as amphetamines; adrenaline and related compounds; a variety of other stimulants, including strychnine; and anabolic steroids.

Amphetamines

Amphetamines are stimulants. During World War II, when they first became available, they were given to German aviators to increase alertness and endurance. The Allied armed forces also used them. For years after the war, amphetamines were widely prescribed for weight loss and other purposes. Some stimulants have been taken for more than one reason. For instance, long-distance runners in the 19th century took opium or sulfate of strychnine to enable them to continue running even when they were in severe pain. One champion bicyclist died from repeated doses.

75

As information about their adverse side effects became available, however, amphetamines came under increasingly tight controls. They are still prescribed for weight loss, narcolepsy, hyperactivity, and a few strictly defined and rare medical conditions. Despite federal regulations on their use, it is believed that a number of athletes are still taking them.

Amphetamines can fight fatigue, but there are several negative side-effects associated with their use. They can cause a weird sort of euphoria that makes an athlete believe he or she has just turned in a world-championship performance when the opposite is true. An athlete on amphetamines has a feeling of split-second timing but in fact has diminished reflex capacity. Amphetamines also increase the risk of serious injury by making athletes oblivious to pain. They make athletes more vulnerable to heatstroke. And they can be addictive.

Amphetamine use is rumored to be widespread in both professional football and baseball, although less so now than 10 years

A large black market is believed to exist in steroids, which are used illegally by some bodybuilders and others wanting to increase muscle mass.

ago. In his book, *Out of Their League,* Dave Meggyesy, a National Football League player in the 1960s, charged that trainers routinely handed out amphetamines in the locker room to get players "up" for the game. Many trainers, and even a psychiatrist, have been accused of giving amphetamines to team members.

Players who take amphetamines become unusually aggressive and hostile. There are anecdotes about some professional players who, after ingesting amphetamines, almost knocked down locker-room doors to get to the opposing team. After the game, this "up" feeling gives way to one of exhausted depression. It is difficult to verify those allegations because athletes do not take urine tests for amphetamines.

Antianxiety Drugs

Also grouped in the category of performance-enhancing drugs are antianxiety drugs. Benzodiazepine, a minor tranquilizer, depresses the limbic system, the center of emotions in the brain. Valium is the most well known drug of this type. Other familiar brand names are Librium, Serax, Tranxene, and Dalmane. Benzodiazepine is thought to be popular in concentration sports such as archery and golf because it inhibits the effect of anxiety-provoking stimuli in the brain. Nonetheless, the benzodiazepines can induce states of intoxication; habitual users of tranquilizers may suffer from diminished psychomotor abilities without being aware of it. Moreover, these drugs also carry a risk of addiction.

Steroids

In amateur athletics, it is now routine to test for the hormones called anabolic steroids, which athletes take to increase muscle mass. Anabolic steroids are effective in achieving that goal; an official position paper of the American College of Sports Medicine says, "The gains in muscle strength achieved through high-intensity exercise and proper diet can be increased by the use of anabolic-androgenic steroids in some individuals."

But the same paper adds that these steroids "do not increase aerobic power or capacity for muscular exercise." And it adds that the drugs "have been associated with adverse effects on the liver, cardiovascular system, reproductive system, and psychological status in therapeutic trials and in limited research on athletes."

77

Anabolic steroids are synthetic versions of male sex hormones. As early as the 1930s, researchers reported that male sex hormones could help build muscle mass. The first effective synthetic anabolic steroid, 19-nortestosterone, became available in the 1950s. Several other synthetics that build muscle mass as effectively as natural sex hormones but have fewer effects on the reproductive system were quickly synthesized, and athletes began using the drugs almost immediately.

It is now recognized that steroid use, which is legal only by prescription, has dangerous side effects. It has been linked to cancer of the liver and to increased risk of heart disease and stroke. There is a large black market in steroid sales, mostly through mail order, because few licensed sports physicians will prescribe them in light of their harmful effects.

Nor are anabolic steroids free of reproductive side effects. In men, they can reduce the size of the testes and lower the sperm count. In women, the steroids can reduce the level of female sex hormones, interfering with the menstrual cycle. In the 1960s, there were continual rumors that the impressive achievements of women athletes from certain countries, East Germany for one, were based in large part on sophisticated use of anabolic steroids. Those suspicions, while never confirmed, remain.

The psychological effects of the abuse of anabolic steroids have been termed *bodybuilder's psychosis* because this syndrome has been observed in athletes such as weight lifters who take large amounts of the hormones. In 1987, physicians at Harvard Medical School said 9 of 31 athletes taking anabolic steroids reported psychiatric symptoms, including hallucinations, paranoid delusions, and manic episodes. "The frequency of psychotic symptoms and manic behavior seen in this small population—all but one of whom were using doses of steroids as much as 10 times greater than those used in any clinical studies done to date—suggests that 'bodybuilder's psychosis' may be a large but covert health problem," the researchers wrote.

Dr. James A. Wright, an army physician at Fort Benjamin Harrison in Indianapolis, cites the 1986 case of a 26-year-old navy aircraft mechanic who took massive doses of anabolic steroids to prepare for bodybuilding competitions. Under their influence, he committed three acts of arson or burglary. A court found him guilty but, because of the massive doses of steroids he had taken, held that he was not criminally responsible. He was placed in a treatment program.

Professional and amateur sports have taken different approaches to steroid use. The National Collegiate Athletic Association has a random-testing program in effect, although it has been challenged in court. The National Football League, in which steroid use is said to be rampant, is sometimes accused of not doing enough to test for steroids. Use among professional athletes is believed to be highest among football players because weight and strength are essential for them.

The long-term effects of anabolic steroid use are not known. Doctors worry that they may be particularly harmful in teenagers, whose bodies are still developing, although there have been no studies to prove or disprove those concerns. A controlled study of former college players and power lifters who regularly used steroids began in 1987 at Pennsylvania State University; it may answer some of the many questions about the damage anabolic steroids are suspected of doing.

DRUGS FOR PAIN RELIEF

Exactly how the body feels pain is not clearly understood. What is known, however, is that certain classes of drugs are able to blunt the body's ability to feel pain. There are three main classes of these drugs: local anesthetics, anti-inflammatory drugs, and narcotic analgesics.

Local Anesthetics

When a basketball player sprains an ankle or a football player strains a muscle in his thigh, simply applying a cold compress often helps alleviate the pain. In the 1980s aerosol sprays, which evaporate very quickly and remove excess heat, are often used to accomplish the same thing. Both methods temporarily cool the skin and provide short-term relief.

Sometimes trainers try to allow athletes to compete even if the players feel pain before a game starts. To do this, they sometimes resort to injecting the player with anesthetic drugs such as Novocain and Xylocaine. These drugs, which are injected directly into an injured joint or muscle, temporarily block the body's

Sean Kelly of Ireland, a favorite in the 1987 Tour de France bicycling race, receives an ethylene glycol spray treatment by a medic after a collision. A fractured shoulder forced him out of the race.

feeling of pain in the specific area in which they are injected, but they can be dangerous. In large doses they can cause convulsions and death.

Anti-inflammatory Drugs

There is available to the sports physician a whole family of drugs used to treat pain and inflammation. There are literally dozens of oral drugs, developed primarily for arthritis, called NSAIDs, for nonsteroidal anti-inflammatory drugs. (The distinction arises because steroids also have anti-inflammatory properties.) Aspirin is the first member of the family. Another, ibuprofen, was approved for over-the-counter sale in 1986 and is available under a number of brand names, including Advil and Nuprin. All the prescription anti-inflammatories have more side effects than aspirin; many affect kidney function and cause dizziness, blurred vision, and stomach problems. One painkiller that is not an anti-inflammatory is acetaminophen, better known under the brand name Tylenol. It is as effective against pain as aspirin but is less widely used in sports because it has no effect on inflammation.

Anti-inflammatory drugs can have the valuable secondary effect of preventing further injury as they reduce pain. Part of the pain involved in a swollen tendon, for instance, is the tendon rubbing against the bone. By decreasing inflammation, the drugs allow injured tissue to heal by decreasing pressure and chafing.

One NSAID that has generated a great deal of controversy is phenylbutazone, stronger than aspirin and often called "bute" after the brand name Butazolidin. Arguments abound over the use of bute in horse racing; the drug is allowed in some states, banned in others. Trainers say prolonged use of bute can destroy a horse because the drug masks the pain that would cause the animal to slow down, preventing severe joint damage. In humans, who may take it for arthritis or bursitis, its use has been known to cause dizziness, diarrhea, and water retention; prolonged use has caused anemia and stomach ulcers.

The strongest class of the anti-inflammatory drugs is the corticosteroids. Cortisone is the most well known drug in this class. Related to the anabolic steroids in chemical makeup, cortisone is a synthetic derivative of similar substances found in the body and is used principally to ease joint pain.

The painkiller "bute" (short for phenylbutazone) is thought to be used widely in racehorses and is used by some humans, too. Its use without a prescription is illegal.

Several years after Dick Butkus retired as a linebacker for the Chicago Bears, he sued the team for a million dollars, claiming that the large number of cortisone shots he had been given caused permanent disability to his knee. Butkus won his case.

As the Butkus case showed, the benefits of cortisone are outweighed by potentially disastrous long-term damage. One major danger of cortisone injections is that although they allow athletes to "play through their pain," by masking the extent of an injury they may drastically compound it. For example, it is believed that basketball player Bill Walton missed years because a cortisone injection, administered to him during an NBA playoff game in 1978, enabled him to play with a serious injury. After the injection, he returned to the game but had to be taken out after several minutes, when the pain became unbearable. Later, X rays showed that he had suffered a broken bone after the injection.

Hall of Famer Sandy Koufax retired early with elbow damage. The cortisone shots he received for arthritis may have hastened the deterioration of the joint.

Moreover, overuse of such injections actually causes deterioration of the affected area and can in fact weaken the joint, leading to reinjury and arthritis. Also, use of corticosteroids may lead to severe hormonal problems once the drug supply is stopped. People who have used these drugs are often unable to fight off infection. In women the drugs may cause abnormal hair growth and menstrual difficulties. The frequent cortisone injections received by Sandy Koufax, the Hall of Fame Dodger pitcher who suffered from severe arthritis of the elbow, are believed to have shortened his career.

Narcotic Analgesics

Drugs in this class of painkillers are derived from opium and include codeine, morphine, and heroin. These potent painkillers achieve their effects by depressing the central nervous system, blocking pain messages to the brain and spinal cord. Both morphine and heroin are highly addictive; morphine may be used for pain relief by prescription only, and even the medicinal use of heroin has been outlawed altogether in the United States. Codeine, on the other hand, is relatively nonaddictive and may be permitted, under some circumstances, for therapeutic use by athletes.

THE SPORTS ESTABLISHMENT RESPONDS

Overall, it has to be said that the reaction of the sports establishment to drug use has been checkered. The strongest steps have been taken against use of street drugs such as cocaine. Both major baseball leagues and the National Basketball Association have programs that allow players to come forward for rehabilitation but ban them for repeated offenses. The National Football League has not yet developed as thorough a program on street-drug use but seems to be moving in that direction. The National Hockey League has no mandatory testing for any of the stimulant or performance-enhancing drugs; it has, however, become concerned of late with alcohol abuse among its players.

Policies about misuse of prescription drugs such as anabolic steroids and amphetamines are even spottier. Professional leagues have largely ignored the issue. American and international amateur sports associations have instituted testing programs, but it is not known how effective they have been in curbing drug use. The root of the problem is the belief that winning is the single object of sports, no matter how that victory is achieved. That attitude leads athletes to find ways to beat the testing programs— for example, by switching from injectable steroids to oral forms that are cleared from the body faster. As long as winning is regarded as more important than competing fairly, drugs will remain a problem in sports.

The treatment of sports injuries with surgery, rest, rehabilitation, or drugs gets a lot of attention, but as in every other medical specialty, the ideal of sports medicine is prevention. And as in most branches of medicine, the patient—the athlete—rather than the doctor is ultimately responsible for taking preventative measures.

•   •   •   •

CHAPTER 7

. . . .

PREVENTION AND FITNESS

The notion of prevention encompasses the whole range of topics discussed in this book. Whereas some preventative measures are best handled by a doctor, other measures are dictated by common sense. Yet any recommendation is useless to the person who is not in shape, for half the battle of prevention is getting fit and staying fit without incurring injury along the way.

Injuries cannot be avoided entirely. That is especially true in professional sports because of the stress that high-level athletics puts on the body. It is estimated that one of every five high school football players will suffer an injury. But almost *every* professional player in any sport will experience injuries, both because

Fifteen minutes is sufficient warm-up time before most athletic endeavors.

they make more demands on their bodies and because an injury that a weekend participant can play with will cripple the pro. At every level of sports there are sensible measures that can deter serious injury or prevent minor injuries from turning into major ones.

FITNESS AND CONDITIONING

The importance of good conditioning and warmups was illustrated by the National Athletic Trainers Association's 1987 study of injuries among female players on high school basketball teams. The study found that 23% of the players had been injured at least once. It also found that almost twice as many injuries occurred during practice as during a game and that 60% of the game injuries occurred in the second half. The trainers concluded that a five-minute warmup period before the second half would reduce those injuries, and, in general, better conditioning programs would reduce the overall number of injuries.

The study also found that three-quarters of the injuries sustained healed in seven days or less. Although many sports injuries are minor enough to be handled by resting or by cutting back a bit on training, many athletes turn a minor injury into a major one by thinking that nature will take care of it or by returning to action before they should.

Every training program begins with a warmup, the first purpose of which is to increase flexibility by stretching the muscles. Stretching starts more blood flowing to the muscles and makes them and the tendons longer. A tight muscle or tendon is more likely to snap than a stretched one. Stretching not only reduces muscle tension but also increases the range of motion and promotes blood circulation. Proper stretching before a workout or competition takes at least 10 or 15 minutes. The postworkout period of stretching is important, too—muscles that have just been put to the test should be given a chance to ease back down to a resting state, in much the same way they are primed before the workout.

There are a number of stretching exercises, each designed for a different set of muscles. Experts note that it is possible to cause injury by overdoing stretching exercises. They recommend a gradual start, with the guiding rule being to avoid any exercise that causes pain. There are great individual differences from one person's muscle tightness to another's —some people are naturally less limber than others. Tight-muscled individuals need more stretching but still will not get as limber as loose-muscled people.

The overall purpose of a warmup is to get the body ready for the stress of exercise. Walking is how most runners do that; throwing is how baseball players do it. The idea is to use the same muscles that are about to get an intense workout, starting with a minimum level of effort, then building toward maximum output. The workout program should depend on what level of performance is the eventual goal.

The American College of Sports Medicine (ACSM) lists four factors that influence the body's response to training:

1. How often you exercise (frequency).
2. How strenuously you exercise (intensity).
3. How long you exercise (duration).
4. What kind of exercise you do (mode).

Based on a number of studies, the ACSM makes these recommendations for the four factors:

1. Frequency: exercise three to five times a week.

2. Intensity: achieve 60 to 90% of your heart's maximum heart rate during exercise (a rough measure for maximum heart rate is to subtract your age from 220).
3. Duration: exercise for 15 to 60 minutes at a time.
4. Mode: do any "endurance activity," such as running, hiking, swimming, or skiing, that uses large muscle groups, that can be maintained continuously, and that is rhythmical.

Depending on the sport, a specific training method will go a long way toward preventing injury. For example, one way to head off some fall-induced injuries is to practice falls, borrowing from the methods of judo; injuries from getting hit, as might occur in football or field hockey, are harder to fend off, though good balance and strength help minimize the potential damage. Training for most athletes, however, centers around flexibility because the most common injuries, and the most easily prevented, involve minor pulls, tears, and sprains.

Isotonic and Isometric Exercise

Exercise can be categorized by the two body functions it affects. Isotonic exercise raises the level of cardiorespiratory fitness; isometric exercise increases muscle strength. Most athletes, professional and amateur alike, engage in both forms of exercise and, indeed, most sports and workouts call both forms into play.

The purpose of isotonic exercise is to increase the ability of the heart to pump blood, the lungs to absorb oxygen, and the blood vessels to carry oxygen-bearing blood throughout the body. For Americans in general, there is great emphasis on cardiorespiratory fitness because diseases of the heart and blood vessels are the nation's leading killers. That is why most sports medicine recipes for fitness focus on the cardiorespiratory angle.

A different set of rules applies if the goal is to increase muscular strength. This is attained by a different type of exercise, isometric exercise, which increases the strength, flexibility, and endurance of the musculoskeletal system. Swimming is an example of isotonic exercise, whereas weight lifting is an isometric exercise (although it includes some isotonic elements).

Isometric and isotonic exercises have strikingly different effects on the body. When you run, swim, or do any other isotonic exercise, your heart beats considerably faster and pumps more blood, your blood vessels widen, and your blood pressure goes

Swimming, classified as an isotonic exercise because it improves the heart's blood-pumping capacity, is an excellent path to fitness. Cardiovascular health is the keystone of overall fitness.

up, but only slightly. When you do an isometric exercise, such as stretching a spring, your heart beats a little faster and pumps a little more blood, but your blood vessels narrow and your blood pressure goes up. If you do enough isometric exercise, your muscle mass increases and so does your muscular strength, but you may not do much good for your heart, lungs, and blood vessels.

The point is not that one kind of exercise is better than another. It is that each kind of exercise has its own value and should be selected with that value in mind, always keeping overall fitness as the goal.

Some Myths About Fitness

There are still many myths about exercise and fitness, despite the increased attention we now pay to our health. One is that strenuous exercise is not good for women because they supposedly are not built for it. That kind of thinking, which kept long-distance running events for women out of the Olympics until the 1980s, is now rare. Today women athletes participate in a full range of sports, with no more medical problems than most men have. They also set marks that once were thought impossible. When Johnny Weissmuller (who later played Tarzan in the movies) won the 400-meter freestyle swimming event in the 1924 Olympics in 5 minutes and 4 seconds, he was hailed as a superman. Women college swimmers now swim faster in training.

It is true that menstrual irregularities have been found in some highly trained women athletes. The onset of menstruation can be delayed in girls who participate in strenuous sports (or other strenuous activity, such as ballet dancing) before puberty. Menstrual irregularities, generally minor, have been reported by many women athletes, but it appears that menstrual function returns to normal when intensive training ends. There is evidence that

Isometric exercise such as weight training builds muscle tissue. Most athletes should combine isotonic and isometric training.

the extremely low body-fat content of highly trained women athletes is related to the menstrual irregularities and that weight gain restores the normal cycle. On the positive side, a Harvard University study has found that women college athletes have a lower rate of breast cancer later in life, apparently because exercise can increase the production of sex hormones that block breast cancer.

A myth with a lot of popular support contends that running increases the risk of heart attacks. People who use that argument to explain why they do not exercise often bring up the case of Jim Fixx, the author of a best-selling book on running, who died of a heart attack while jogging in 1984. In fact, Fixx was a former smoker whose family had a history of heart disease and who had ignored his own symptoms of heart trouble. He did not take the precautions advised by sports physicians for a man with his medical record.

Doctors who have studied the relationship between sudden death and exercise in middle-aged men—those in the high-risk age group for heart attacks—have come up with fascinating findings. It is true that the chance of having a heart attack goes up during running and other kinds of exercise, because the heart gets its maximum workout then. In other words, someone who is going to have a heart attack has a greater chance of having it during exercise.

But overall, the researchers have found a lower risk of heart attack among those men who exercise regularly and follow recommended precautions, such as getting a medical checkup before starting to run. The temporary increase in risk during exercise is greatly outweighed by the overall improvement exercise gives.

The argument can easily be turned around. If an out-of-shape man has a higher risk of heart attack during exercise, then the way to avoid a heart attack is not to get out of shape. That means starting an exercise or training program early in life and sticking with it.

Cardiovascular Fitness

What counts for cardiorespiratory fitness, according to the American College of Sports Medicine, is the total amount of exercise. And the right combination of effort multiplied by time spent can be attained in different ways. "If the total energy cost is similar, it does not matter what mode of exercise is chosen; therefore a variety of endurance activities will accomplish the same result," an ACSM position paper said.

The goal of improved cardiovascular fitness is accomplished by aerobic training, which can be anything from brisk walking to swimming to dancing to running. The purpose of aerobic training is to push the body to extend its capabilities but without overdoing it. There are several ways to judge how much aerobic exercise is enough. As a general rule, the intensity should be sufficient to raise a sweat and cause hard breathing but not real shortness of breath. Another recommended method for gauging intensity is to measure the heartbeat during or immediately after exercise. The rough rule of thumb is not to exceed about 75% of the maximum heart rate.

The difference between fitness and flaccidity, between a well-conditioned athlete and a flabby spectator, can be measured easily. The heart of an out-of-shape person who is sitting in a chair beats about 70 times a minute, pumping 5 quarts of blood. The heart of the athlete in the next chair pumps the same amount of blood but beats only 50 times a minute. When the two begin to exercise, the athlete's heartbeat will go up to about 100 a minute, compared to 150 beats for the person who is out of shape. Pushed to the limit, the athlete's heart will pump as much as 30 quarts of blood a minute, compared to 20 quarts for the flabby individual.

If both are hooked up to a machine that measures oxygen consumption, the results tell a similar story. An athlete's body can use up to five quarts of oxygen per minute, compared to less than three quarts a minute for someone who is out of shape. Both are taking in the same amount of air (assuming that neither one smokes or has a respiratory problem), but the athlete's body is better able to use the oxygen. Doctors used to worry about some of the changes that occur with exercise. In particular, the enlargement of the heart seen in highly trained athletes was regarded as a potentially dangerous abnormality. Textbooks used to describe something called "athlete's heart," or "cardiac hypertrophy." It is now recognized that the enlargement is beneficial. The heart is a muscle like any other, and exercise makes it not only bigger but stronger.

The general recommendation is to alternate hard and easy workouts—sessions in which the body is pushed as hard as possible and sessions involving much less stress. The reason is that the body needs time to recover from strenuous exercise—time to replenish its glycogen stores, to allow tiny muscle tears and strains to heal, and to restore body chemicals lost during exercise.

In addition to aerobic exercise, there are also training techniques designed specifically for the muscles. Muscle strength can be increased by weight lifting or other techniques that involve maximum effort for a limited number of repetitions. Muscle endurance can be improved with exercises that involve a limited amount of effort for many repetitions. Muscle training can be done using equipment no more complicated than a set of dumbbells and weights or with complex and expensive machines, of which the best known is the Nautilus.

There are several signs that warn of overtraining. The clearest of them is pain. Persistent muscle stiffness and soreness are also signs of overtraining, but others are more subtle: fatigue, sluggishness, depression, inability to maintain a good level of performance.

The Benefits of Fitness

It has been shown that people who exercise regularly live longer, on average, than people who do not. The most convincing study has been done by Dr. Ralph Paffenbarger and his colleagues at Stanford University, who for decades have tracked nearly 17,000 graduates of Harvard College. Dr. Paffenbarger found a consistently lower risk of heart attack in men who exercised regularly, no matter what their age and other habits. For middle-aged men, the study found that every hour of exercise added two hours of life expectancy.

That study came up with some good news and some bad news for people who hate to exercise. The bad news was that the benefits of exercise cannot be stored. Men who were athletes in college and later gave it up were no better off than men who had never exercised. The good news was that *any* kind of exercise increases life expectancy. If the goal is to live longer, the Paffenbarger study gave an easy formula: Just burn 2,000 calories a week, in any way you like. (Extra energy expenditure above 2,000 calories gave no extra life expectancy.) The way the calories are burned makes no difference.

So if the goal is just to live longer, it can be achieved in any number of ways. You can burn about 300 calories per day (to reach a weekly total of 2,000) by strolling leisurely for 90 minutes

How to Train for a Marathon

Preparing for a marathon is a wholehearted and time-consuming effort, with many rewards along the way.

The marathon is a grueling 26.2-mile footrace that originated nearly 25 centuries ago, when the Greeks were defending their homeland from the invading Persians at the Battle of Marathon. Legend has it that a Greek warrior named Pheidippides relayed news of the outcome by running from the battlefield to the capital at Athens, a distance of about 23 miles. When he reached his countrymen, he uttered the Greek word *nike*, meaning "victory," with his last breath.

The marathon as an athletic event was introduced to the modern world at the 1896 Olympic Games in Athens. The distance varied depending on the layout of the course but was standardized in 1924 at 26 miles, 385 yards. Today, marathoning is a popular sport for men and women. One should, however, consult a doctor before starting to train for such a test.

Training extends over at least an eight-week period. Beginners should build up from a few miles of running per day to a peak of 50 miles per week, taking about a month to reach that plateau; a veteran runner should build up to at least 70 miles per week. All runners should taper down their mileage two to three weeks before race day, in order to let the body and mind rest up from their intensive training and to make them hungry for the race itself.

In one common type of training, called the hard-easy method, the runner alternates hard and easy days. He or she will vary how far, as well as how hard, to run from day to day. For example: In running 8 miles on Monday, 6 on Tuesday, 10 on Wednesday (and so on), the runner pushes the body on the longer runs and gives it time to recover on the shorter runs. Jaunts of 12 to 16 miles generally should be made no more than once a week, the last coming 2 to 3 weeks before race day.

A few runs of 15 to 20 miles are absolutely necessary to prepare a runner for hitting "the wall," a physiological barrier past which one's energy is nearly gone. As a general rule, training runs should not exceed 20 miles (or 3½ hours) because too much exertion severely depletes the body and can lead to injury. Save the all-out effort for the race.

For many years, it was believed that a marathoner had to train at distances *longer* than the race itself. Then in 1952 the Olympic gold medal was won by a man who had never previously raced more than 10,000 meters (about ¼ the distance of a marathon). Today, most intermediate runners subscribe to the belief that they can run three times farther than their average training distance. So, they try to average eight or nine miles a day.

Variety in the training schedule can be attained in several ways: Run half the daily mileage in the morning, half in the evening; or, run hard-easy. Another way is to introduce speed work into the routine: Run several 880s (the yardage of most oval tracks) at a moderate pace, following each with a 3-minute breather. Still another way is crosstraining: Count miles biked or swum as miles run. Participating in short races or minimarathons will prepare runners for race day and sharpen their sense of competition.

Nutritional needs in the training period will not change greatly from the usual dietary requirements. Most runners consume plenty of carbohydrates and fruit juices. (See Chapter 3 for a fuller discussion of nutrition.)

Replacing fluids is vital. A runner should drink water approximately 30 minutes before going for a run; every 20 to 40 minutes during the run; and after the run, too.

Though this preparation can be demanding, there are many rewards built into a regular running schedule. As the body becomes more fit and the mind becomes sharper, the marathoner can play longer and harder, work more efficiently, eat more healthfully, and sleep more soundly. And the sense of accomplishment grows with each hour spent focusing on the finish line.

Hard workouts can be coupled with lighter workouts to give the body recuperation time. Good conditioning and injury prevention are every athlete's responsibility.

or walking briskly for about an hour; by bowling for an hour and a quarter or raking leaves for an hour; by playing doubles tennis for an hour or singles for 40 minutes; by jogging for 40 minutes or running for 30 minutes.

That daily caloric expenditure is just the minimum. Higher life expectancy does not necessarily lead to better fitness. If the goal is physical fitness, a new set of factors is introduced. The American College of Sports Medicine lists four different fitness categories:

- Cardiorespiratory endurance (the heart, blood, and lung capacity to do extended exercise).
- Body composition (the relative proportion of fat and lean in the body).
- Flexibility.
- Strength.

There may be no one activity that addresses all of these categories equally, but running, swimming, cycling, and some gymnastic events are among the sports that fill the categories best. Among team sports, soccer, hockey, and basketball are among the best for promoting total fitness.

In general, it can be said about prevention that the athlete who knows how his or her body works stands the best chance of keeping it from harm. Overall good health requires attention to diet, warming up, conditioning, and maintaining the right balance between periods of exertion and recuperation—because an overstressed body is much more likely to break down in some way than one in peak shape.

Although almost anyone who exercises or plays sports is susceptible to injury, the emphasis should not be on what can go wrong in athletics. For the well-trained person who follows sensible rules of training and prevention, things will go right. The real successes of sports medicine today are the millions of Americans who lead lives of health and fitness because they know and respect their bodies.

•   •   •   •

APPENDIX:
FOR MORE INFORMATION

The following is a list of organizations that are able to furnish additional information and/or assistance.

Aerobic & Fitness Association of
  America
15250 Ventura Blvd., Suite 802
Sherman Oaks, CA 91403

American College of Sports
  Medicine
(street address)
401 West Michigan Street
Indianapolis, IN 46202-3233
(mailing address)
P.O. Box 1440
Indianapolis, IN 46206-1440
(317) 637-9200

American Physical Therapy
  Association
1111 North Fairfax
Alexandria, VA 22314
(703) 684-2782

Athletics Congress of the USA
200 South Capitol Avenue
Suite 140
Indianapolis, IN 46225
(317) 638-9155

Canadian Association of Sports
  Sciences
333 River Road
Ottawa, Ontario CN K1L 8H9

Joint Commission on Competitive
  Safeguards and Medical Aspects
  of Sports
c/o Donald L. Cooper, M.D.
Director-Chairman
Oklahoma State University
1202 West Farm Road
Stillwater, OK 74078-0625
(405) 624-7026

National Association for Sport and
  Physical Education
1900 Association Drive
Reston, VA 22091
(703) 476-3410

National Athletic Health Institute
575 East Handy Street
Inglewood, CA 90301
(213) 674-1600

National Fitness Association
P.O. Box 1754
Huntington Beach, CA 92647

Nicholas Institute of Sports
  Medicine and Athletic Trauma
Lenox Hill Hospital
130 East 77th Street
New York, NY 10021
(212) 439-2700

FURTHER READING

Darden, Ellington. *The Athlete's Guide to Sports Medicine*. Chicago: Contemporary Books, 1981.

Dominguez, Richard and Robert Gajda. *Total Body Training*. New York: Warner Books, 1980.

Garrick, James G., M.D. *Peak Condition: Winning Strategies to Prevent, Treat and Rehabilitate Sports Injuries*. New York: Crown, 1986.

Goldman, Bob. *Death in the Locker Room: Steroids & Sports*. South Bend, IN: Icarus, 1984.

Meggyesy, Dave. *Out of Their League*. New York: Warner Books, 1971.

Mirkin, Gabe, M.D. *Dr. Gabe Mirkin's Fitness Clinic*. Chicago: Contemporary Books, 1986.

Mirkin, Gabe, M.D., and Marshall Hoffman. *The Sportsmedicine Book*. Boston: Little, Brown, 1978.

Nieman, David C. *The Sports Medicine Fitness Course*. Palo Alto, CA: Bull Publishing, 1986.

Pearl, Bill, and Gary T. Moran. *Getting Stronger*. Bolinas, CA: Shelter Publications, 1986.

Roy, Stephen. *Sports Medicine*. Englewood Cliffs, NJ: Prentice-Hall, 1983.

Shangold, Mona, M.D., and Gabe Mirkin, M.D. *The Complete Sports Medicine Book for Women*. New York: Simon & Schuster, 1985.

Vandeweghe, Ernest M., M.D. *Growing with Sports: A Parent's Guide to the Young Athlete*. Englewood Cliffs, NJ: Prentice-Hall, 1979.

GLOSSARY

aerobic exercise conditioning, such as running, walking, and swimming, that improves respiration and circulation by expanding the blood vessels and increasing oxygen consumption

alternative medicine a group of specialties relying less on surgical procedure and more on holistic or manual healing, including chiropractic, osteopathy, massage, and acupuncture

amino acids the building blocks of proteins; of the 20 amino acids found in humans, 10 must be ingested by a person to maintain health; the remaining 10 can be synthesized by the body

amphetamines drugs that stimulate the nervous system; used illegally to enhance athletic performance; many are legally unavailable without a doctor's prescription; can be addictive

anabolic steroids male sex hormones (usually synthetic) taken to promote tissue growth and weight gain; taken by athletes to increase muscle mass; they work by increasing the metabolic process involved in protein synthesis

anaerobic exercise conditioning, such as weight lifting, that builds muscles without increasing oxygen uptake

analgesics pain-killing drugs (taken internally or applied topically) ranging in potency from aspirin to morphine

anti-inflammatories drugs that reduce swelling and prevent enlarged tissues from chafing against bone by contracting blood vessels; includes Advil, Nuprin, and other brands made from ibuprofen

arthroscopy diagnosis or surgery using a microcamera inserted into a joint

bursitis inflammation of the bursae, fluid-filled sacs inside joints

Butazolidin (called "bute") trade name for phenylbutazone; a drug used for analgesic or anti-inflammatory treatment in bursitis, e.g.

carbohydrate a member of a group of compounds that share a general biochemical structure containing carbon, hydrogen, and oxygen; includes sugars and starch; must be obtained by people though diet; to be metabolized, all types of carbohydrate are broken down into glucose; excess is stored as glycogen or as fat

carpal-tunnel syndrome a condition common to cyclists, in which nerves in the wrist become pinched, causing dysfunction of the hands

cartilage dense connective tissue of three types; depending on the type, may be found lining the ends of bones in joints, providing cushioning from impact, or in such places as the nose, bronchi, external ear, and the intervertebral disks and tendons; has no blood supply and so cannot heal from injury

cortisone a steroid that regulates the change of amino and fatty acids into glucose, also suppresses inflammation of injured parts

fascia sheet of tough tissue covering or binding some body parts; found on the sole of the foot, for example

fat a substance containing one or more fatty acid; the main substance into which excess carbohydrates are converted for storage by the human body

frostbite tissue damage resulting from freezing due to lack of blood circulation; usually occurs in the extremities (fingers, toes, ears, etc.); ice forms within the tissue; frostbitten skin should be warmed in tepid water, not rubbed

glycogen a carbohydrate composed of chains of glucose units; in humans, it is the primary form of carbohydrate storage; fuels muscles

heatstroke a potentially fatal condition characterized by high body temperature, absence of sweating; may lead to unconsciousness due to failure of the body's temperature regulation system; victim should be cooled with damp cloths and given fluids

hydrocollator a pack containing silicon and sand gel that absorbs hot water; used to apply heat to an injured area

isometric exercise conditioning that is based on a system of contracting opposing muscles or contracting muscles against something resistant; increases muscle tone and bulk without shortening the muscles

isotonic exercise conditioning that shortens muscle fibers without greatly increasing their tone; characterized by contracting muscles in the absence of resistance

joint a specialized structure at the junction of two or more bones; most allow for movement, such as the shoulder, knee, ankle, elbow, or wrist

kinesiology the study of the structure and movement of the human body

ligament a dense, fibrous tissue that serves to stabilize and strengthen a joint, linking bone to bone

metabolize to chemically change substances within a living organism in order to release useful energy

muscle fibrous tissue with the ability to produce force or movement; there are three types of muscle; striated—attached to the skeleton, smooth—found in the walls of internal organs and blood vessels, and cardiac—located in the heart walls

musculoskeletal system striated muscles attached to the skeleton and the bones of the skeleton; also includes tendons and ligaments, which link them together

nonsteroidal anti-inflammatory drugs (NSAIDS) medications such as aspirin that relieve pain and swelling; safer than steroids

opiates drugs derived from opium, including morphine, codeine, and their derivatives, such as heroin; they depress the central nervous system and relieve pain; however, because they are addictive, their use should be strictly controlled by a doctor

pronation movement of the hand that turns the palm to face downward, crossing the bones of the forearm

protein compounds composed of amino acids; necessary to form muscles, organs, and tissues, as well as hormones and enzymes; excess protein can be converted to glucose and metabolized

pyruvate-lactate reaction a biochemical reaction that occurs in instances when muscle activity is so extended or so great that there is a lack of oxygen; the glucose or the glycogen being metabolized is broken down into lactic acid rather than the usual end product, pyruvic acid; lactic acid is thought to account for muscle fatigue and soreness

rotator muscle that enables rotation

shin splints a class of ailments denoted by sharp pain in the lower leg caused by overuse and muscle imbalance

spinal cord the bundle of nerves running through the center of the spinal column, serving as a pathway for messages between the brain and the trunk and limbs

tendon a band of strong tissue that connects bones to muscles

tennis elbow inflammation of the tendon at the outer edge of the elbow caused by overuse of the muscles in the forearm, as may occur in tennis

ultrasound therapy the use of high-frequency sound waves projected into injured tissue to break up scar tissue and increase circulation

vertebrae bones that compose the backbone, 33 in an infant, 26 in an adult; bound together by ligaments and intervertebral disks

vitamin one of a group of substances required by the body but not able to be produced by it; must be ingested to maintain health

INDEX

PICTURE CREDITS

Edward Edelson, author of *Nutrition & the Brain* and *Drugs & the Brain* in Chelsea House's ENCYCLOPEDIA OF PSYCHOACTIVE DRUGS, is science editor of the *New York Daily News* and past president of the National Association of Science Writers. His other books include *The ABCs of Prescription Narcotics* and the textbook *Chemical Principles.* He has won awards for his writing from such groups as the American Heart Association, the American Cancer Society, the American Academy of Pediatrics, and the American Psychological Society.

Dale C. Garell, M.D., is medical director of California Childrens Services, Department of Health Services, County of Los Angeles. He is also clinical professor in the Department of Pediatrics and Family Medicine at the University of Southern California School of Medicine and visiting associate clinical professor of maternal and child health at the University of Hawaii School of Public Health. From 1963 to 1974, he was medical director of the Division of Adolescent Medicine at Children's Hospital in Los Angeles. Dr. Garell has served as president of the Society for Adolescent Medicine, chairman of the youth committee of the American Academy of Pediatrics, and as a forum member of the White House Conference on Children (1970) and White House Conference on Youth (1971). He has also been a member of the editorial board of the *American Journal of Diseases of Children.*

C. Everett Koop, M.D., Sc.D., is Surgeon General, Deputy Assistant Secretary for Health, and Director of the Office of International Health of the U.S. Public Health Service. A pediatric surgeon with an international reputation, he was previously surgeon-in-chief of Children's Hospital of Philadelphia and professor of pediatric surgery and pediatrics at the University of Pennsylvania. Dr. Koop is the author of more than 175 articles and books on the practice of medicine. He has served as surgery editor of the *Journal of Clinical Pediatrics* and editor-in-chief of the *Journal of Pediatric Surgery.* Dr. Koop has received nine honorary degrees and numerous other awards, including the Denis Brown Gold Medal of the British Association of Paediatric Surgeons, the William E. Ladd Gold Medal of the American Academy of Pediatrics, and the Copernicus Medal of the Surgical Society of Poland. He is a Chevalier of the French Legion of Honor and a member of the Royal College of Surgeons, London.